ENCYCLOPÆDIA METROPOLITANA:

OR,

System of Universal Knowledge:

ON A METHODICAL PLAN

PROJECTED BY SAMUEL TAYLOR COLERIDGE.

SECOND EDITION, REVISED.

First Division.   Pure Sciences.

MORAL AND METAPHYSICAL PHILOSOPHY.

MORAL AND METAPHYSICAL PHILOSOPHY.

PHILOSOPHY OF THE FIRST SIX CENTURIES.

BY

THE REV. FREDERICK DENISON MAURICE,

CHAPLAIN TO LINCOLN'S INN;
PROFESSOR OF ECCLESIASTICAL HISTORY, KING'S COLLEGE, LONDON.

SECOND EDITION, REVISED.

WIPF & STOCK · Eugene, Oregon

Wipf and Stock Publishers
199 W 8th Ave, Suite 3
Eugene, OR 97401

Moral and Metaphysical Philosophy
Philosophy of the First Six Centuries, Second Edition, Revised
By Maurice, Frederick D.
ISBN 13: 978-1-60899-711-4
Publication date 7/22/2010
Previously published by Richard Giffin & Co., 1854

PREFACE.

THE first part of this treatise on Ancient Philosophy was published, in a separate form, three years ago. I said in the preface to it that the second part must be entirely rewritten, the original draft in the Encyclopædia being as unsatisfactory to the writer as it could be to the readers of it. I did not at all know, at that time, what a task I was undertaking, or how much the difficulties of it would be increased by the brevity I had imposed upon myself, and by my determination to give only what I had originally projected—a sketch of the progress of thought—not a report of systems, which would save the student of them from the necessity of referring to Brucker or to Ritter. Considering how poor the result is, I am ashamed to confess how much trouble it has cost me to fix the form and method of the treatise, or how often the preliminary portion of it has been recast. I have no doubt that many will think I have been more diffuse than my limits warranted; that many will complain of me for neglecting writers whom I ought to have noticed; that the two classes of critics will agree in the opinion that I have always chosen the wrong occasions for compression or for dilation. I can only say that I have endeavoured to present faithfully what appeared to me the aspect of each period; that I have intentionally passed over those who I thought (rightly or wrongly) did not illustrate its character; that I have tried to make those who did, speak for themselves, not (so far as I could help it) through any modern interpreter.

As the task has been pursued in the midst of some not congenial occupations, I have accomplished far less than the publisher had reason to expect. The present part is an instalment : it embraces six very important centuries. I trust I may be able more successfully to seize the characteristic points in the Philosophy of the Middle Ages, and in that which connects them with our own time.

HAY, SOUTH WALES:
September 1853.

CONTENTS.

	PAGE
INTRODUCTION	1–4
FIRST CENTURY	4–18
Seneca	4
Epictetus	9
The Jews	14
The Christian Teachers	16
SECOND CENTURY	19–38
Plutarch	19
Emperor Trajan	23
Ignatius of Antioch	24
Saturninus	26
Justin	29
Emperor Marcus Aurelius	31
THIRD CENTURY	38–81
Numenius the Pythagorean	39
Tertullian	42
Pantænus	45
Clemens of Alexandria	45
Ammonius Saccas	54
Plotinus	55
Porphyry	68
Abammon or Iamblichus	71

CONTENTS.

		PAGE
FOURTH CENTURY		82–114
Constantine		82
The Arian Controversy		84
Athanasius		85
Julian		85, 90
Augustin		96
FIFTH CENTURY		115–139
Proclus		116
Boëthius		138
SIXTH CENTURY		139–157
Emperor Justinian		140
Pope Gregory I.		148

INTRODUCTION.

1. IN the sketch of Ancient Philosophy, we spoke of different nations which were busy in the search for Wisdom. The Hindoo enquired whence the Thoughts which he found within him, whence the mysterious power of thinking, had flowed. The Chinese found it hard to regulate his outward acts: he asked for some Rule or principle of Conduct. The Persian perceived a war in himself and in the world between two powers, one of which should be obeyed, one resisted: he sought for the meaning of Good and Evil. The Greek felt in himself a power of Governing men who were physically stronger than himself: he asked what this power was, and how he became possessed of it. The Roman perceived that there was an Order to which he, and all persons, and all things must conform: he asked what that Order was,—what place he and other men had in it. *The Philosophy of the Old World.*

2. Out of these questions, others arose which made the solution of the first more difficult. The philosopher of each nation or race, whatever was the motive which led him to commence his search, aimed at some one object or principle. The pursuit of Unity, or the one, became formally and consciously with some, really with all, the absorbing pursuit. But the traditions of each nation had preserved the belief of many objects demanding the reverence of man. How to respect these traditions, and yet faithfully to engage in that pursuit, became in every country a most perplexing problem. The more earnestly men investigated the problem with a real desire to solve it, and to fulfil what they felt to be the duty of their lives, without forsaking their respect for their fathers and their love for their land, the more they felt the embarrassment. If they endeavoured to be citizens as well as sages, to teach and act as well as think, the freest and most tolerant of all states was most likely to *Its Perplexities. (1) Unity and Polytheism.*

condemn them as corrupters of youth, and despisers of the Gods.

(2.) The Invisible and Visible World.

3. Another difficulty was inseparable from this. The philosopher evidently sought for something not visible, not tangible. The source of Thoughts must be as impalpable as themselves. The outward acts and forms of life might be worthy of the most minute and devout observance, but the Rule which was at the root of them could not be one of them. The evils which he saw led the disciple of Zoroaster to crave for a Good which he could not see. The very difference of the Greek from other men was, that his Power did not lie in that which had bulk, and could be measured. The Roman Order was reverenced as that which surmounted all visible power and authority. Hence the material world, with which men generally seemed to be occupied, was certainly not that with which the seeker was occupied. He was looking into some other. What had that world to do with this? Were they under the same law, or under different and opposite laws? So long as the philosopher occupied himself as Confucius, Zoroaster, Pythagoras, Socrates, Plato, Aristotle did, with the actual conditions of society, he must try, by some means or other, to reconcile the two spheres, to show that he was investigating the laws which concern the ordinary life of men. To point out the method of this reconciliation,—to prove this fact, was the business of his life. But there was latent in the minds of all these eminent thinkers a feeling which frequently expressed itself in their words and acts, that the region with which the philosopher had to do was in fact altogether opposed to that with which the common man had to do. With all his practical zeal, the Persian reformer could not overcome the habitual conviction of his countrymen, that an evil power had created the visible universe. With all his wish to prove that justice or righteousness is equally at the root of society and of individual life, Plato could not sometimes help thinking that the philosopher must have an Atlantis, not an Attica, to work in. The theoretic man was the object of Aristotle's profoundest admiration, in spite of his large and minute acquaintance with the facts of the earth on which he moved, and his deep interest in all the concerns of it. That belief which Persians and Greeks in their vigour could not escape, was the original and unchanging maxim of the contemplative Hindoo. For the most opposite reason, it became also the maxim of the active Roman, when he began to receive philosophy from the lips of Stoics, Academicians, and Epicureans. The fixed and long-established forms of his national life withstood the application of any new discoveries. When those

forms decayed, and the vulgar strife of factions absorbed the toils of the most accomplished men, so far as they were statesmen and men of action, they welcomed speculation as a delightful region into which they might escape if ever they could exchange the noise of the forum for their villas and gardens. Cicero laboured diligently to bring his rhetorical and political views into harmony with his philosophical. But the contrast between them became more and more evident even to himself. The administration of such a Republic as Rome could have nothing to do with studies which he had conducted, or fancied that he had conducted, in the school of Plato.

4. But if there was a world for the philosopher, and a world for the common man, how was the philosopher distinguished from the common man? Hindoos, Persians, Greeks in the time of Pythagoras even in the time of Socrates, would have said,—" The philosopher is an inspired man. Some divinity has taken him out of the crowd, and brought him to know secrets which the crowd does not know." Much temptation to vanity and imposture lay of course in this belief; nevertheless, those who held it were less, not more, exclusive than their fellows. Their sympathy with their disciples was cordial and fraternal; they felt that light was given them that they might descend into the darkness to bring others out of it. Philosophical pride really began when this conviction departed. The Sophists and the heads of the Latin sects felt that they were different from other men, not in virtue of gifts and a calling, but in virtue of their own native endowments. In proportion as philosophy became a profession, the whole race of non-philosophers—that is to say, all mankind, except the school or its chief members—were regarded with contempt, or with indifference, if so strong a feeling as contempt was incompatible with the sage's ideal. *(3.) The Philosopher and the Man.*

5. It may naturally be supposed that the difficulties of which we have spoken presented themselves in a new light to the philosopher under the Roman Empire, especially under the first twelve Cæsars. The seeker for Unity found the habits, rites, Gods of all nations, adopted into the same society: if *this* reconciliation was that which he aimed at, his object was attained. He found all the nations subjected to one head: if *this* was unity, his problem was resolved in the most practical manner. What effect would it produce on the Roman seeker after Order, to find himself and his law subjected to a mortal will? How would the Greek search for government, and freedom thrive, when the Greek found himself a slave? Would there be the dream in any heart, that the Gods bethought themselves of a world which Tiberius or Nero governed,—that such a world could have a moral and metaphysical foundation? *How did the establishment of the Roman Empire affect these inquiries?*

4   L. ANNÆUS SENECA.

The first century.

6. The records of the first century of the Christian Era furnish interesting and valuable answers to these questions. They give us clear and full portraits of a Roman and a Greek Stoic, with an unfinished sketch of a reformer and enthusiast in whom many Greek and Oriental qualities were mingled; they supply us with other facts, sometimes supposed to have no connection with a history of philosophy, which throw light upon these, and are necessary to the comprehension of the ages which follow.

Seneca born a few years B.C.; died A.D. 65.

7. LUCIUS ANNÆUS SENECA was born in Cordova. He inherited from his father, Marcus Seneca, a considerable property, and a great aptitude for rhetorical studies. There was much in his education which might have led him to think the enlargement of his fortune and the study of words the main business of life. But Seneca became a Stoic. He proposed to himself the acquisition of inward contentment and self-satisfaction as his end; he looked upon philosophy, not the courts, as the means to that end. He was, however, a Roman before he was a Stoic. A pedantic contempt for wealth formed no part of his profession; if he could make it minister to his main object, he was quite willing to hold it and increase it. It separated him from the vulgar; it allowed him leisure for self-cultivation. He was as little anxious to alienate the other part of his patrimony from any notion that barrenness and dryness of style are necessary or becoming in the seeker of wisdom. He early found that the forum was not the place in which a subject of the Cæsars was likely to realize the blessings which he especially desired; but the gifts which qualified him for the forum might, he thought, be applied advantageously in the closet.

His wealth and Rhetoric not inconsistent with his Stoicism.

8. The contemporaries of Seneca, of course, were quick in detecting what seemed to them the gross contradiction of a Stoic dwelling in some of the finest gardens in Italy, and patronized by an Emperor. Later times have been more busy in their complaints of Seneca for his points and antitheses. Neither, we conceive, have been just to him. He worked out the problem which Zeno had set before his disciples, with as much consistency as any of them had ever done. But he worked it out in new circumstances. He tried to show that the material objects in which other men placed their happiness, did not necessarily hinder a philosopher from attaining that which specially belongs to himself; that equanimity was possible in the midst of a society liable to hourly changes from the will of a tyrant. His style may be called artificial, but it is the perfectly natural expression of the mind of the man who used it. No other could enable us so well to understand the continual

effort which he was making to keep himself steady while all was reeling about him; the skill with which he availed himself of all resources for this purpose; the degree in which he was able to subordinate all other purposes to it. If self-concentration, independence of mere circumstances, independence of other men and their interests, an assertion of the position of the philosopher as immeasurably higher than that of the ordinary man, be stoical aims and characteristics, Seneca was in the very strictest sense of the word a Stoic. He was a Stoic, too, in his reverence for physics. A brilliant essayist and historian of our day has alleged him as the most damning proof of the inutility and barrenness of moral studies; his Treatise on Anger being contrasted with those beneficial investigations of nature which have led to the construction of various necessary and marketable articles. Seneca himself might have been quoted in support of this opinion, though he exalted natural above human studies, not on the ground of their utility but their sublimity. He valued even the knowledge which he could acquire of meteors and volcanoes above all theories about Indignation and Consolation. It may seem strange that so prolific a writer on ethics, and one who connected ethics so much with the practice of life, should have taken such a view of the relative worth of these pursuits. But, in truth, Nature furnished him, as well as other Stoics, with their ethical standard. How nearly they might approximate to its fixed order,—how far they might cast aside the disturbing forces of impulse and affection, was their question. Seneca went farther in finding the answer to it than any of his predecessors. His Treatise on Anger is no mere collection of well-turned sentences: it exhibits an ideal of character which he set before himself habitually, and which it cannot be denied that in a great measure he realized. The miseries and oppressions of the earth did not disturb his peace. The crimes of the palace never led him to dream, as an old Athenian might have dreamt, of Harmodius; or to pray, as an old Roman might have prayed, for a divine avenger; or to mix, like his kinsman Lucan, reverence for Pompey and Cato with adulation of Nero. He was not inspired, as Juvenal was in a somewhat later time, by mere indignation, to pour out verses. He did not brood, like Tacitus, over the inevitable fall of his country's glory when its virtue had departed, nor anticipate the possible greatness of the untamed tribes in the forests of Germany, because traces of old Roman virtue were to be seen in them. Seneca was as much offended as so mild a man could be, by the dangerous sentiment of Aristotle, that anger, though a bad master, is a good servant. It is bad, he said, altogether. He disposed rapidly and decisively of the objection that moral evil ought to

His preference for physics.

See the Preface to the Nat. Quest. lib. i.

How accounted for.

His calmness.

De Irâ, lib. i. § ix.

excite the displeasure of a philosopher, by urging that the philosopher in Rome who began to act upon that maxim must be displeased all day long.

De Irâ, lib. ii. § vii.

9. Whatever subject Seneca handled is treated in this spirit. Some extracts from his fragment on the Rest of a Philosopher, addressed to Gallio, will illustrate the tone of his mind and of his style. The reader will not fail to observe that the two republics of which Seneca speaks in it explain *his* idea of the philosopher's own world. It is not the ideal republic of Plato into which he would transport himself, but into the largest conception of this visible universe which he can frame.

Treatise De Otio. Sapientis.

After some general comments on the blessings of retirement as a deliverance from the influence of opinion,—from the distraction of different objects,—from the fluctuations and inconstancy which characterise us even in our vices,—Seneca proceeds to defend himself from a charge which he had perhaps heard from Gallio himself, to which, at all events, he must have known that he was liable from rival professors.

c. xxviii. and xxxi.

"You will say to me, 'Seneca, what do you mean ? When you praise idleness in this fashion you are deserting your party. Your friends the Stoics say, 'Even to the very end of our lives we will be acting ; we will not cease to work for the common good, to aid individuals, to stretch out a kind hand even to our enemies. We grant freedom from service to no age ; as the saying is, we keep the hoary head pressed with the helmet. We are so impatient of rest before death, that, if it were possible, we would not have death itself a rest ! Why do you mix the precepts of Epicurus with the principles of Zeno ? If you are ashamed of your party, why not desert it rather than betray it.'"

Allegation of Epicurism.

Seneca answers that he does not hold himself pledged to all the sentiments of Zeno or Chrysippus ; that he is a seeker of truth as well as they ; that, however, he has not deserted either their principles or their example. "The two great sects," he says, " of Epicureans and Stoics differ in this matter, but they arrive at my conclusion by different routes. Epicurus says a wise man will not take part in the management of the state unless there is some special reason for doing so ; Zeno says he will take part in the state unless there is some special hindrance. One seeks rest of purpose, the other from necessity. But the necessity has a wide scope. If the Republic is so corrupt that it cannot be aided,—if it is completely possessed with evils,—the wise man will not spend his strength for nought ; he will not devote himself to a task in which he can do no good. As a man would not go to sea in a damaged ship,

Coincidence of Zeno and Epicurus.

—as he would not enter military service when utterly out of health,—so he will not enter upon a political life which he knows to be untenable. No doubt it is demanded of him that he should do good to many men when it is possible,—if not, to a few—if not, to those nearest to him,—if not to them, then to himself. But if a man makes himself worse, he hurts besides himself, all those whom, if he had been made better, he might have benefited. So if any one deserves well of himself, he does thereby good to others, in that he puts himself in a condition to do them good. *Political life.*

" Let us present to our mind," Seneca continues, " the two different societies,—one, that great republic in which gods and men are contained, in which we do not look at this corner or that, but measure our city by the course of the sun; the other, that in which the condition of our birth hath enrolled us. Some devote themselves at the same time to both societies, the greater and the less; some only to the less; some only to the greater. To this greater republic we may be servants even when we are at rest,—yea, I know not whether we cannot serve it better at rest." *The two states. c. xxxi.*

He goes on to mention some of the exercises in which a contemplative man may engage. "He may ask, What is virtue? Is there one virtue, or are there many? Is it nature or art that makes good men? Is this a great unity which embraces seas and lands, and whatever is in them? or hath God scattered through the Universe many bodies of the same kind? Is the matter from which all things are sprung, full and unbroken? or is it dispersed, and a void intermixed with the things that are solid? Doth God sit still in the contemplation of his own work; or doth he meddle with it? Is He diffused beyond it, outside of it; or doth He inhabit the whole of it? Is the world immortal; or is it to be reckoned among perishable things, —things born for time"...... *Questions for the contemplative man.*

Seneca proceeds, in an eloquent passage, to show what a multitude of objects Nature forces upon the mind of man; how she stirs him up to acts of contemplation, for which the time allotted to his life is all too short. Therefore he concludes—"I live according to Nature if I have given myself wholly to her,—if I am her admirer and worshipper. 'But Nature,' you say, 'would have me both act and have leisure for contemplation.' I do both, since contemplation implies action. 'But,' you say, 'surely it makes a difference whether one comes to this work for the mere sake of pleasure, seeking nothing from contemplation but itself, which, however purposeless, no doubt has its seductions. I answer," he says, "it also makes a great difference with what spirit you *c. xxxii.* *Contemplation and action.*

engage in civil life,—whether it is that you may always be in a bustle, and never have any time left in which you may withdraw from human things to divine. The mere craving for action, and doing works for their own sake, is not to be approved, any more than the virtue which is wholly contemplative and never exhibits what it has learnt. With what mind does a wise man withdraw into leisure?—That he may ascertain with himself what things he is to do by which he may benefit those that come after. "I affirm," he says, "that Zeno and Chrysippus did greater things than if they had led armies, had borne civil honours, had laid down laws for *one* state, instead of laying them down, as they have done, for the whole human race."

Both may be pursued for bad or good ends.

He argues that the supporters of pleasure and of action both recognise the necessity of contemplation; he, on his side, does not affirm that it is the ultimate port, but only a place for lying at anchor. "A man, according to Chrysippus, may not only suffer but choose rest. The Stoics lay it down as a general rule that he should concern himself in the affairs of the State, but they do not admit that he should concern himself with *every* State. Will you tell me, then, which it shall be? Shall it be the Athenian, in which Socrates was put to death and Aristotle had to fly lest he should be condemned? Shall it be the Carthaginian, in which there were perpetual seditions, the liberty of which was dangerous to every good citizen,—where there was inhumanity towards enemies, hostility to friends? If I chose to go through them one by one, I should not find one which could suffer a wise man, or which a wise man could suffer. But if that state does not exist which we feign for ourselves, Rest begins to be necessary for all; because the one thing that might have been preferred to Rest is nowhere. If I am told that it is an excellent thing to go out to sea, but that I must not for the world sail in a sea in which shipwrecks are wont to happen, which carry the steersman where he would not go, I think I am told plainly enough never to loose my ship from shore, though sailing is so excellent a thing."

Republics too bad to mend.

Conclusion.

10. With the philosophical habits and convictions which this extract discloses, Seneca was called to form the mind of an emperor. His Treatise on Clemency, addressed to his pupil, is probably a fair illustration of the method of his education. The royal youth is reminded how like his position is to that of the gods, how many millions are subject to his nod, how graceful and divine kindness and forgiveness must be. Objections to the value of a quality which presumes transgression are dexterously suggested and dexterously taken off. Nero is congratulated that he is exhibiting in the commencement of his reign,

Seneca the tutor of Nero. Treatise De Clementia. c. i.

c. ii.

—in the hey-day of his passions,—all the noble qualities which his predecessor, Augustus, only acquired after a series of crimes. How great will be the maturity of excellence of which the first buds are so beautiful!

11. It may not be fair for an Englishman, with Bacon's dedication of the "Advancement of Learning" before him, to complain of the pagan parasite; it may not be fair to look upon the life of him to whom the "Treatise on Clemency" was addressed, as a commentary upon it and upon the views of the writer. But if the tutor is not answerable for the acts of his pupil, what must be said of his own? Though we may admit that the censure of Dio Cassius upon the tenor of his life is malicious and false,—though we may even force ourselves to believe that the evidence of his privity to the death of Agrippina is not conclusive,*—no one has ever doubted that he wrote the apology for the matricide. Which crime was the greater must always remain a question. Forgiveness has been asked for this and other acts of the philosopher, on the plea that he was exposed to temptations under which we might any of us have fallen. We do not say that the atrocity of the offence is an answer to such an argument; certainly every one would wish to accept it on behalf of a man who has so many claims upon our gratitude as Seneca. But, before it can be admitted, there should be some evidence of weakness, of reluctance, of shame. None such are produced. We have not the least reason to conclude that Seneca felt he was departing from the maxim on which his life was regulated in this instance, any more than when he submitted quietly and manfully to the sentence upon himself. He had tutored himself to endure personal injuries without indulging in anger; he had tutored himself to look upon all moral evil without anger. If the doctrine is sound, and the discipline desirable, we must be content to take the whole result of them. If we will not do that, we must resolve that it is well to hate oppression and wrong, even at the cost of philosophical composure.

Margin notes: Crimes of Seneca. See especially Dio. Cass. lib. 61. c. 10. Tacitus, Ann.lib.xiv. c. 12. Not the effects of weakness.

---

12. EPICTETUS inherited no gardens, and learned no rhetoric; he was the slave of a freedman of that emperor whom Seneca educated. The difference in their position affects the whole nature of their philosophy. They were both Stoics; they had both a right to the name; they both redeemed Stoicism from schoolmen and nurses, and gave it a manly, practical character. But

Margin notes: Epictetus the seeker of freedom. He lived till the reign of Hadrian; but was driven from Rome as a philosopher by Domitian.

* The words of Tacitus, Ann. lib. xiv. c. 7, only leave it uncertain whether Seneca and Burrhus knew of the first plot of Anicetus; the completion of the crime our philosopher seems to have suggested.

10   HIS MAIN OBJECT AND PRINCIPLE.

Epictetus. Seneca inquired after the secret of quietude,—Epictetus after the secret of freedom. The poor Greek slave in the Roman empire applied himself to the study of that problem which the sophists, poets, statesmen of Athens, had been working out in the days of Pericles : what is more, he found a solution of the problem which justified all the aspirations of old Greece, and explained their failure.

13. Viewed in this light, Epictetus becomes one of the most striking figures in the history of philosophy. He has thrown back a glory upon the early Stoicism which does not belong to it; his influence upon men's thoughts in later times has been very considerable; what he has said upon the subject to which his whole mind was devoted, had never been said in language so distinct and brave by any Greek or Roman prede-
The philosopher and the man one. cessor. But the real grandeur of his work consists in this, that he broke down the barrier which Seneca, and the comfortable men of letters before and since his age, have been always seeking to establish and perpetuate. The man and the philosopher are not different persons with him; the sole business of the philosopher is to ascertain how he can be most a man. It was not a question, how he could acquire a certain amount of wisdom which would set him above his fellows; it was the ques-
His philosophy altogether practical. tion, how he could live when all his circumstances seemed to bid him die. "Thou art a slave:" that was the fact presented to him by his outward condition. "What makes thee one?" was the thought awakened in him. "Is it Nero? Is it fate? Is it God?—None of the three," was the reply which by degrees came to him. "Not Nero, for he is a slave as well as thou; not fate, for thou art not bound to be a slave; not God, for He would not have thee a slave:—it is thyself. Thou fanciest that all these things, the accidents which surround thee, over which thou hast no power, are necessary to thee: therein consists thy slavery. When thou ceasest to desire these things, and desirest to be what thou art meant to be, thy freedom begins."

Book i. chap. 1. What the gods give men power over, and why. 14. Here is his view of the state of man and the divine purpose respecting him :—It will be perceived that he limits the omnipotence of the Gods by a kind of necessity; but that he desires to assert their Righteousness at all events.

"The gods have made that which is highest of all, and which is the lord of the rest, alone dependent upon us,—namely, the right use of the objects which are presented to us; but other things not. Is it because they were not willing? I, for my part, think that, if they could, they would have committed even those things to us.........But what saith Jupiter? 'Oh, Epictetus! if it had been possible, I would have made that

HUMAN GREATNESS—BROTHERHOOD.

little body of thine, and that which thou possessest, free and unencumbered. But do not forget that this is not yours; it is only a little mud skilfully moulded. Seeing I could not do this, I gave thee a portion of that which belongs to us—the power of desiring and declining,—the power of pressing into action and turning from action,—and, in general, the power of using the images that are presented to thee; of which power if thou takest care, and placest thy well-being in it, thou wilt not be hindered or interfered with, thou wilt not groan, thou wilt not complain of anybody, thou wilt not flatter anybody.'"

Here is his view of human greatness, and the ground of it:—
"If anyone hath been able worthily to enter into this doctrine,—that we are in some very eminent sense born of God,—that He is the father of men and of gods,—I do not think that he will have any grovelling or mean thoughts of himself. If the Cæsar had adopted thee, how proud thy looks would be! and if thou knowest that thou art the son of Jove, will not that elevate thee? It is not so with us, however; for these two things have been mixed in our birth,—the body, which is common to us with the animals; the reason and the mind, which are common to us with the gods. Many decline to that unhappy and dead relationship, while only a few ascend to this godly and blessed one. Seeing, therefore, it is needful that every person whatsoever should use each thing according to his conception of it, those few who think that they are born to faith, and to modesty, and to safety in the use of the images that are presented to them, cannot judge meanly of themselves. But the majority cry, 'What am I?—A poor miserable little creature;' and 'This miserable flesh and bones of mine!' Miserable enough, no doubt; but you have something better than that flesh and these bones. Why, then, letting the worse go, have you not cleaved to the better?" *Book i. Chap. 3. Men's relationship to Jupiter.*

The following extract is perhaps even more remarkable :—
When a certain man asked him how it is possible to eat in a manner well pleasing to the gods, "If it is possible," he said, "to eat justly, with an even mind, temperately, modestly; is it not possible also to eat in a manner pleasing to the gods? When you have asked for warm water, and the servant does not hear, or, having heard, brings it a little tepid, or does not happen to be in the house, not to be angry or break out,—is not this pleasing to the gods? 'But how can one bear such things as these?' Poor slave! will you not bear your own brother, who hath Jove for his author,—who, as a son, hath sprung from the same seed and the same divine generation? Because you have been cast on some place which is a little higher than another, will you straightway set yourself up as a tyrant? Will you not *Book i. Chap 13. How to please the gods in common things. Ground of patience.*

remember who you are and whom you rule,—that they are kinsmen, brothers by nature, Jove's offspring? 'Aye, but I have paid for them, and they have not paid for me.' 'Do you not see where you are turning your eyes,—that it is to the earth, to the pit, to those miserable laws of the dead; while to the laws of the gods you have no regard?"

How to read Epictetus. 15. We have taken these extracts almost at hazard from Arrian's reports, which are, on the whole, more valuable, because freer and more human, than the Enchiridion. They explain the grand maxim of Epictetus, the one which lay close to his heart, which he had tested and knew to be true. We shall utterly fail to understand him if we make a digest of his opinions upon ethics, physics, theology; or busy ourselves with inquiring which were derived from older authorities, which were original. He derived nothing from older authorities, if to derive means to receive as part of a traditional system. There was nothing in his philosophy original, if by original is meant that which is invented as an easy method of explaining the phenomena of the Universe. Epictetus needed to be free. Any one who would show him how he might take a chain from off his neck, was welcomed as a benefactor. But he knew that no precepts can break fetters which we forge for ourselves. Stoicism became transformed in his hands, not because he wished to alter it, but of necessity; one who craved freedom for his spirit as its first condition, must give a new aspect to doctrines which prescribed a stern submission to fate. Yet he did not contradict his masters,—he understood them better than they understood themselves. He asserted as strongly as they did, that the course of the world is under a law which man cannot alter; it is his folly and calamity that he is always complaining of things which are independent of him. He asserted as much as they could do, that man himself is under a law. Why does not he obey it, and so cease to be a slave of things which have no rightful dominion over him?

He was not a plagiarist nor an inventor.

His theology. 16. So with respect to the theology of Epictetus; it could not be any longer physico-theology, such as Chrysippus had promulgated. The world could not be God, nor could he worship a collection of world-gods. There was an eye over him; he wanted a divine power to help him against the things which were trying to crush him. Seneca, in his gardens, conceived of a distant Omnipotence, of which the Emperor was the living and practical image; Epictetus, the bondsman, came to believe in One to whom a suffering man might look up for help and deliverance.

THE PYTHAGOREAN REFORMER. 13

17. Supposing there was this possibility of freedom and greatness in man, was it possible that the multitude of slaves, rich and poor, in prisons and high places, could be awakened to seek for emancipation? How, and by whom, should they be awakened? These thoughts appear to have occupied Epictetus scarcely more than they occupied Seneca; but there were philosophers in this time who aspired to be reformers, not of themselves only, but of their age. The figure of APOLLONIUS of Tyana floats dimly before us in the traditions of the third and fourth centuries, when he had been changed into a model hero, and when his name was needed for a polemical purpose. But that there was such a man in the first century, and that he indicates some of the stronger feelings that were at work in it, cannot, we think, be doubted. His biographer, Philostratus, belongs to the time of Septimius Severus. The distance of less than 150 years is not so great that we need suspect any mistake in the assertion that Apollonius conceived an early admiration for Pythagoras, and a desire to do for his own generation what he supposed the old sage had sought to do for his. Pythagoras, as we have seen, was distinguished from the later teachers by the assured conviction of a divine inspiration; by the acknowledgment of an invisible power to be served in silence and awe as the source of that inspiration; by the belief that it was to be used for the reformation of society. Apollonius seems to have felt strongly the difference between such a philosophy and one which belongs to the schools, to be used for the purpose of endless disputation. He felt even more strongly the difference between the worship which Pythagoras had encouraged among his disciples, and that worship of evil powers to be propitiated by sacrifices, which was kept alive by the priests of various nations and gods, in the Roman and Parthian empires. That a young man should encounter many of these priests, should have proclaimed the pure philosophical devotion which he supposed to be the substitute for their dark rites, is not, surely, an impossible, even an improbable, supposition. It is more consolatory to think Philostratus true than false, when he affirms that supposition to be the fact. That he could not have entered upon his gigantic task without a sense of a calling which he had learnt from Pythagoras to regard as the characteristic of a sage, and that he prepared himself for it by the methods of silence and purification which his master prescribed, we may also believe. That the sense of the impossibility of any radical change in the faith of men and the order of society without a divine power should have grown upon him as he proceeded, was most natural. The statements of his idolatrous admirers compel us to think that he ultimately identified these powers with

Dreams of reformation.

Apollonius of Tyana.

His admiration for Pythagoras.

Opposition to priests.

Sense of inspiration.

14   THE JEW IN ALEXANDRIA.

An enchanter.

himself; used the gifts which he had, and the opinion of his mission, for selfish and dishonest purposes; practised the ordinary tricks of the enchanters, who were then everywhere so numerous. The admission of this fact does not oblige us to question the sincerity of his original purpose, to deny that a better Wisdom than his own stirred him, as it stirs every reformer, with a sense of the evils of his time, and a passionate desire to cure them. Nor need we be at pains to refute his conclusion, that some mightier agency than any which the philosophers or priests of his time were dreaming of, must be at work to renew the universe.

Relation of the Jews to philosophy.

18. There was one nation now reduced under the power of the Cæsars, which had stood in a different relation to philosophy from all the rest. The Jew was not pledged by his faith to reverence the multitude of sensible objects which interfered with the search after Unity; he was pledged to protest that they were no gods, and to refuse them worship. The search after Wisdom did not contradict, in his apprehension, the fact that the Divine Wisdom had revealed itself to him : the more earnest his conviction on the latter point was, the more vigorous and continuous did his search become. The belief that the seeker of Wisdom was inspired, that he could not seek unless Wisdom first sought him, was therefore deeply rooted in his mind. But the seeker was also the prophet who was to communicate; he could claim no part of his knowledge as his own; his privileges were those of an Israelite; he could have no greater.

Reference to the Alexandrian school.

19. We have seen that an Alexandrian teacher living under the Roman Government during this century, understood the advantage which his Jewish birth gave him, and asserted his right on the strength of it to pursue Wisdom himself, and to sympathise with the efforts which other men had made in various directions to pursue it. Instead of condemning the Gentile philosophers, he referred their light to the same origin as his own. Philo, whom we spoke of as in some sense winding up the philosophy of the old world, does also in a very important sense introduce the new. We shall have to trace his influence through several centuries, not in his own city, or among his own countrymen only. Yet Philo, we saw, regarded the philosopher almost as Seneca regarded him. Chosen by God, separate from other creatures, he has feelings, interests, hopes, in which common men are not intended to share. How can so zealous and enlightened an Israelite have wandered so far from the principles upon which the commonwealth of Israel stood ? Evidently, because he has lost the sense of it as a com-

monwealth; its homely facts have become allegories; the history has evaporated into a philosophy.

20. A strong practical protest against the Philonic tendency, still more against the mixture of Jewish with Heathen wisdom, arose from the sect of the Pharisees. This sect could not be accused of sacrificing the outward to the inward, of converting letters into symbols, of substituting spiritual contemplations for authoritative dogmas. But they were as little historical as the Alexandrian school. Tradition stood with them for history; the living records which make the past a part of the present, were exchanged for dead customs and rules, which make the present merely the slave of the past. The past itself was the indistinct echo of human voices; God was not heard in it. A school of self-righteous men was as far removed from sympathy with those who bowed to its decrees, confessed its divinity, hated its inhumanity, as the professors of the most occult lore, the aspirants after the most divine communion. *The Pharisee.*

21. The Sadducee was a philosopher like the Alexandrian, but in the most opposite sense. For him there was no invisible world. He scorned the formalities of the Pharisee, but he substituted for them formalities of another kind,—maxims of conduct, the proprieties and decorums which separate the easy and respectable from the multitude, the sagacity and experience which separate the civilized from the unlettered. Some have called him an Epicurean, some a Stoic; he may at times have resembled both; he had no natural affinity with either. His sacred books supplied him with the hint of a morality which is higher and deeper than all ceremonies and services; he had only to separate this morality from all relation to any powers and influences beyond the visible world upon which it was to be exercised, and there came forth a system compact and manageable enough for all ordinary uses, capable of putting forth some vigour as long as it had anything not more vital or substantial than itself to fight with, turning that vigour into ferocity when it had. *The Sadducees.*

22. If philosophy is the pursuit of Unity, it was as little likely to thrive amidst these divided sects, as in any countries which nominally professed a divided worship. The hard dogmatism of the Pharisee made all search fruitless and profane. The dogmatism of the Sadducee kept enquiry within limits, which nearly every philosopher of the old world had felt it the first duty and necessity of his vocation to transgress. The idea of spiritual guidance and inspiration, formally recognised by the one, contemptuously denied by the other, was equally alien from the heart and intellect of both. It was incompatible with the slavish reverence which the one paid to *Both opposed to Philosophy, in any real sense.*

the dead letter of the sacred books, and the comments of the elders upon it,—with the confidence which the other had in his own intellect, with his assurance that there could be nothing of which it did not give him information.

The Christian Gospel why apparently opposed to Philosophy.
23. It would seem at first as if the proclamation which called forth all the jealousy and bitterness of both these schools, was even more opposed to philosophy than they were. For it was a proclamation. Those who made it called themselves heralds, not seekers. They said they had news for their nation and for mankind of that which actually was, not hints of that which might be. They spoke of a revelation of a hidden world, and of Him who ruled it,—not of a method of discovering it or Him. This language is even more characteristic of the cultivated Saul of Tarsus, than of the Galilean fishermen; there is a more strong assertion in his writings than in theirs, that the wisdom of the world must stoop to the folly of preaching. What could be expected of such a faith, but that it should treat all the questions with which philosophy had been occupied as vain, or that it should pronounce decisions upon them so definite and precise, as to make past enquiries obsolete, future enquiries needless or rebellious?

It touches upon all the questions of Philosophy.
24. The Christian teachers were not able to take the first course; for the Gospel which they preached treated of all the questions in which philosophy had been engaged, and proclaimed them to be of transcendant importance. The thoughts and movements of the mind and heart within, were as profoundly interesting to the preacher of the cross, as they could be to the Brahminical devotee. The acts which he does in the common relations of life are as much connected with his faith as they can be with that of the Chinese. All the facts which he believes refer to the conflict between Good and Evil, and to the question which is to triumph. How spirit is to be free from the control of that which is merely material, and shall exercise dominion over it, is a subject as carefully discussed and elaborated by St. Paul as by Plato. The announcement of a divine and spiritual Kingdom, which was the primary subject of the new Gospel, at once appealed to all that desire for an Order by which the Latin was possessed.

The Christian could not oppose Thought and Search without abandoning his position.
25. The Christian Church did not therefore occupy a ground of its own, different from that on which the philosopher had been working: it was his own ground. He had a right to say that it was invaded. The Christian abandoned his position if he denied the charge. He abandoned it equally if he took up the other plea, and affirmed that he was furnished with certain propositions which entitled him to put down the thoughts

that were stirring in the minds of men already,—to prohibit the rise and growth of them. For he came declaring that the eternal God who had made man in His own image, had sent forth His Son to regenerate human society and human life in its first root, and that His Spirit was given to men to awaken them out of a dead sleep into a knowledge of their position as men, into the apprehension and enjoyment of a spiritual world—a kingdom of righteousness and truth. Everything, then, of torpor and death was at war with this faith, and with Him who was the object of it. All desire, striving, effort, however confused and likely to be abortive, was recognised as originating in a divine source, was capable of being organized and directed to a divine end.

26. Already during the first century all the principles of this faith had been developed. It had come forth in an actual society. It had encountered the Sages of the Athenian marketplace, as well as approached the palace of the Cæsars. But it was still regarded, by both sages and Cæsars, as the most insignificant of the numerous sects of the most turbulent province and incomprehensible religion of the empire, till the capital of that province and religion fell before the army of Titus. Then it came forth in a new character: separated from all local associations, denounced by the race from which it had sprung, it called upon all races of which the Roman Empire was composed, to acknowledge the God of Abraham. It affirmed that an actual kingdom, grounded not upon strength, but upon submission and sacrifice, was existing in the midst of those races; that all might claim the King of it, as their King; that an actual invisible power had come forth, and was at work to unite them in this fellowship. Such assertions had their political, as well as their popular and their philosophical side. Emperors, mobs, sophists, were equally bound to take notice of them. We are not anxious to force this conflict upon the notice of our readers; but it forces itself upon them even more when they are reading the civil history of Gibbon, than when they are reading the ecclesiastical histories of Baronius or of Mosheim. The historian of philosophy can pass it over less than either of them. For five centuries it presents itself in different forms to his notice. If those five are disregarded, the thirteen which follow become unintelligible. Upon this subject we now enter. The Christian Scriptures treat the years previous to the destruction of Jerusalem, or the death of the last apostle, as the winding up of a period, rather than as the commencement of one. The same arrangement of epochs is suggested by the circumstances of the Roman Empire. The reign of Vespasian seemed to his contemporaries to mark a new

The Church in the first century.

New position in the second.

Its place in a History of Philosophy.

THE ORDER OF THE HISTORY.

The first century transitional. epoch. Domitian's reign revived the dark times of Tiberius and Nero. With Nerva an age commences which Gibbon rashly calls the happiest in the annals of the world; and which, though famines, pestilences, wars, rob it of that honour, is certainly illustrated by a series of princes who stand in the most marked and brilliant contrast to the Cæsars of the first century. We are justified, therefore, in treating that century as transitional, belonging equally to the old world and to the new. The new world we divide into three periods. The first will embrace the years which elapse between the commencement of the reign of Trajan, and the appearance of Mahomet.

PART I.

FROM THE REIGN OF TRAJAN TO THE APPEARANCE OF MAHOMET.

CHAPTER I.

THE SECOND CENTURY.

FROM TRAJAN TO SEPTIMIUS SEVERUS.

1. THE distinction between the Greek and Latin provinces of the Roman Empire becomes more strongly marked while other distinctions disappear. The two languages, by whomsoever they were written or spoken, seem always to denote two essentially different habits of mind. The great Latin writers after Seneca did not cease to be philosophical, but they ceased to be formal professional philosophers. Tacitus felt that it was a more truly Roman work to study the actions of men and the condition of empires, than to acquire the art of being unaffected by either. Quinctilian felt that he was a truer patriot when he was doing his best to prevent rhetoric from becoming a trade, by making it a science, than if he had used his rhetoric in the construction of moral theories and apopthegms. On the other hand, the great Greek writers who followed Epictetus all testify that his thoughts had taken the direction which was most strictly in accordance with the language which he used as his instrument. They might derive great benefit from their Roman position and their Roman masters; but the tongue of Plato and Aristotle, now especially that it was no more claimed by poets, was the natural inheritance of those who made the search after wisdom the end of their lives. *Greek and Latin languages.*

2. There was one writer of this time who clearly understood that this was the vocation of his countrymen, but who perceived also, more clearly than his predecessors or any of his cotemporaries, that the Greek mind and the Latin mind at this time were needed to sustain and illustrate each other. To this conviction we may fairly attribute the great services which Plutarch of *Plutarch of Cheronæa.*

Cheronæa has rendered to mankind. It must have struck many as a puzzling fact, that they owe the strongest and most vital impressions which they have respecting the freest ages of Athens and of Rome, to a writer who lived under Domitian and Trajan. The obvious suggestion, that at no other time could the lives of the heroes of each country have been so well compared, is a help to the solution of the difficulty, but does not remove it. Plutarch could not have understood enough of either to compare them, if he had not united some of the higher qualities of both. He saw in the old Roman the domestic affection, the reverence to invisible powers, the subjection to law, which were the strength of the commonwealth, the loss of which was its destruction. His beautiful letter to his wife on the death of their child, his practical treatises on all, even the minutest parts, of education, his eagerness to vindicate the old forms of religion from the dark and malignant superstitions with which they had been mingled, show how much pains he had taken to train himself to those habits which did not belong to the land of his birth. But the passion for liberty, the love of the soil, the eagerness to discover the principle that lay beneath outward facts, were as obviously the causes of the past glory of Greece, the witnesses of its present degradation. The interest which Plutarch compelled himself to feel in politics when all politics seemed to have passed away, his amusing vehemence against Herodotus for his libels upon Bœotia, and his efforts to understand the old philosophers, show how thoroughly and heartily he was determined to make his extraneous education a means of bringing out more fully the sympathies and powers which belonged to the countrymen whom he celebrated.

Union of Greek and Roman qualities in him.

3. Only this combination could have enabled Plutarch to be what he has been to modern Europeans, and to Englishmen, through Shakspeare, more than to all others. It has been the ungrateful fashion of some modern historians to speak of him as an uncritical retailer of anecdotes; it has been still more the fashion with philosophers to treat him as a man without originality, the mere reproducer of opinions which greater men had held. The former pedantry is harmless enough if it does not prevent children from reading Plutarch: were it to have that effect, our interest in classical antiquity would speedily disappear; we should have a set of old heroes clad in unexceptionable costume, not a single feature remaining which marks them as individual men. The other affectation is connected with the doctrine which has been so widely diffused among the historians of opinions, that a man's thoughts are good for nothing till you can ascertain to what school they belong, and that they must have been copied into his mind from books, if

Objections to him as uncritical and as a plagiarist.

he shared them with any more ancient teacher. Plutarch, instead of being a mere copyist, was, it seems to us, one of the great restorers of life and originality to philosophies which had become utterly dead. His genial habits of mind, his historical spirit, his affectionate study of actual men, enabled him to appreciate thoughts and feelings which some even of the great teachers of the world had been unable to grasp. Aristotle, we have seen, though living so near the time of Socrates, could not in the least understand him; for him he was merely a teacher of Ethics, so standing in contrast with his pupil, who dealt with Theology and Physics likewise. In the schools of the Academics, full of disputation as they were, the great disputer and confuter was utterly misrepresented,—the object of his life inverted. Cicero apprehended him only through Xenophon, or through some of those splendid passages of declamation in Plato which exhibited least of the master's character. To Seneca he must have been an exceedingly disagreeable object, always suggesting some topic to disturb the equanimity which a sage desires. But Plutarch, in his "Platonic Questions," entered at once into the subtlest essence of the Socratic teaching,—that which belonged to the spirit of the man himself, and in which lay the secret of his power. Why, instead of boasting of his art as a generative one, he called it obstetric; why he thought that the deepest wisdom was not invented, but recollected; lastly, how the Dæmon gave the meaning to all the deepest thoughts which he uttered, so that his philosophy never could be understood apart from it,—these are points which Plutarch handles more courageously and successfully than they perhaps ever have been handled before or since his time, because he felt more to Socrates as a learner and as a friend, than as a panegyrist or a critic.

<small>His work as a philosopher.</small>

<small>His understanding of Socrates.</small>

4. If Plutarch holds a most important place as the reviver, in the truest sense of that word, of lessons which had been mistaken or had become obsolete, he is not less important as the foreteller of a new philosophical era. From his time it became quite clear that the age of the old sects had passed away. We do not mean that Epicuræans, Stoics, and Academicians, might not go on maintaining their different theses and collecting bands of disciples around them; such occupations or amusements, if less animating than the games and shows in the amphitheatres, were also less expensive and less bloody. But the discovery that these questions meant something to the men who engaged in them in the old world,—that they bore upon their business, that they had to do with the most serious struggles of their lives,—inspired thoughtful men with a disgust for the abuse of them to mere purposes of talk or display, and

<small>Assists in overthrowing the sects.</small>

THE INWARD TEACHER.

Plutarch. with a hope that there might yet be treasures lying very close to human beings which they had not discovered, and of which *His practical wisdom.* they did not suspect the existence. And secondly, no one did more than Plutarch to prove that, in some way or other, the old belief in divine helpers, protectors, inspirers, must be connected with the search for practical wisdom,—with all our efforts after self-knowledge and self-government. He may not have succeeded in showing how the reconciliation was to be effected; but, at least, he makes us aware of some of the difficulties which lie in the way of it; and he leaves us in no doubt that whosoever stifles man's questionings for the sake of asserting a divine authority, blackens and blasphemes that authority; that whoever seeks to carry on such inquiries without referring them to a deeper source and a superior guidance, makes them feeble and abortive.

His " Dæmon of Socrates." 5. We should be glad, for other reasons, to give our readers a sketch of the dialogue, which is entitled "The Dæmon of Socrates," though only a small portion of it bears directly upon that subject. But there is one passage so important, not for the illustration of Plutarch's mind, but of the whole philosophical movement of this time, that we must translate it:—

Not a visible appearance. " When we considered this question privately among ourselves, the suspicion suggested itself whether it was a visible appearance at all which Socrates spoke of, whether it might not be the sensation of some voice, or rather the intellectual recognition of a word coming, in some wonderful manner, into contact with him, as even in sleep it is not a voice that is uttered, but those who receive the impressions and perceptions of certain *His speech not addressed to the external ear.* words think that they hear people speaking. To these, this kind of apprehension is in very deed a dream, coming to them in the silence and serenity of the body while they sleep. [There is a word lost in the next sentence, which leaves some doubt about its meaning.] And having been stifled with the tumult of the passions and the whirl of outward necessities, they cannot listen and address the mind fully to the things which are signified to *The purified spirit the true listener.* them. But the reason of Socrates being pure, not under the dominion of passion, nor mixing itself greatly, under the pretence of outward necessities, with the body, was quick and sensitive in responding to that which encountered it; and this, one would conjecture, was not the *voice*, but the *word* of a dæmon coming in its signification, without voice, into contact with the perceiver. For the voice, when we speak with one another, is like a blow upon the soul, which opens by force to receive the word through the ears. But the reason of the better man leads the well-matured soul, which needs no blow, directing it to that which has been internally signified to it;

and it permits itself to be guided by the light gentle reins which the reason uses,—no violent passions champing the bit, and striving to be loose."

6. The student of philosophy will do well to consider the whole passage, from which this is an extract, attentively. It will afford him great light respecting the distinction between αἴσθησις and νόησις, which is of such vast importance for the understanding of the earliest as well as the latest metaphysics. Scarcely less valuable are the suggestions which the passage offers respecting the relation of the Νοῦς to the ψυχή, of the teaching governing power which apprehends spiritual objects directly, to that receptive faculty or principle which may be either the victim and slave of the senses, or may obey a higher guidance. But it is especially needful to remark, that both these vital distinctions depend in Plutarch's teaching upon the precious acknowledgment of some Dæmon or Spirit, who addresses itself to an organ in man capable of communicating with it, and to which that organ must yield itself freely if it fulfils its proper function. He does not profess to define the faculties (the beautiful language which he was using, not with the perfect freedom and mastery of an old Greek, but perhaps with even a more critical apprehension of its powers and distinctions, almost forbade him to do so) apart from the power which moves them, and the object to which they are directed. *The important distinctions in this passage.*

7. It may be doubted whether the Emperor Trajan, to whom Plutarch dedicated his "Sayings of Kings and Generals," ever troubled himself to read the dialogue on the Dæmon of Socrates. In spite of his cultivation, he was probably too much occupied with Dacian conquests, and the internal management of the Empire, to have much time for what would have seemed to him ingenious and somewhat difficult speculation. He was, therefore, the less prepared to encounter a new and very startling form of the doctrine of an inward teacher and guide, which was presented to him when he came to the city of Antioch, on his way to an expedition against the Parthians. The ordinary policy of the Empire, the habits of toleration which accorded with the character of Trajan and which his intercourse with Pliny had nourished, would have forbidden him to interfere with any strange opinion, whether it took the shape of religion or philosophy. Under his benignant despotism, all schools might deliver their separate and contradictory oracles,—all races whose rites were not outrageously inhuman, might worship their separate gods according to the traditions of their fathers. But Trajan heard of a society in Antioch, which his very tenderness *The Emperor Trajan.*

His tolerant maxims.

TRAJAN'S DIALOGUE WITH IGNATIUS.

Apparent exception to Trajan's rules.

Grounds of it.

for the feelings and faith of its volatile inhabitants led him to regard with dislike and suspicion. He understood that the members of it drew men away from the worship of their native and proper gods, proclaiming, as the humbled Jewish nation had done, one invisible Ruler of the whole earth, but inviting men of all tribes, as the Jews had not done, to abandon their divinities, and unite in confessing Him. He found that these men spoke of themselves as parts of a kingdom; a phraseology altogether different from that of any sect or school. It might have been the mere phraseology of harmless fanaticism; but there was evidently an organization in the Antioch community; one, called a father, presided over it; it was connected by mysterious bands with societies similarly organised in the other cities of the Empire. To suppress such a body, as outraging the religion of Syria, as interfering with the polity of Rome, was a most natural course for the Emperor to adopt. He sent for Ignatius, the father of the Society or Family, which was called Christian, in Antioch. It is to his conversation with this father that we must for a moment direct the attention of our readers.

Ignatius of Antioch.

The evil spirit.

The divine teacher.

The deliverer.

8. "When Ignatius stood before the face of Trajan the king,—'Who art thou, poor devil,' said the Emperor, 'who art so wilfully transgressing our decrees, and moreover art tempting others to their destruction?' Ignatius answered, 'No one calleth him who bears a God within him a poor devil, for the devils turn away from the servants of God. But if thou meanest that I am evilly inclined towards the devils, and that I give them trouble, I confess it. For having Christ as my heavenly King, I set at nought the plots of these evil spirits.' Trajan said, 'And who is this that beareth a God within him?' Ignatius answered, 'He that hath Christ in his heart.' Trajan said, 'Seem we not in our minds to have gods, seeing that we use them as allies against our enemies?' Ignatius said, 'The devils of the nations you call gods through a mistake. For there is one God that made the heaven, and the earth, and the sea, and one Christ Jesus the Son of God, the only begotten: of whose kingdom may I be a sharer!' Trajan said, 'Thou meanest Him who was crucified under Pontius Pilate?' Ignatius said, 'Him who hath crucified my sin with the author of it, and hath put down all devilish error and evil under the feet of those that bear him in their heart.' Trajan said, 'Dost thou, then, bear this crucified One in thyself?' Ignatius said, 'Yea, verily, for it is written, I will dwell in them and walk in them.' Trajan exclaimed, 'We decree that Ignatius, who saith that he beareth the crucified One within him, be led bound to Rome, there to be the food of wild beasts.'"

9. We have hesitated to introduce a passage at once so theo- How this logical and so sacred as this; but it is impossible faithfully to dialogue bears upon exhibit the history of Christian, or even of heathen, philosophy, the history during the first three centuries, if we pass it over. Even if we of philosophy. had any doubt about the substantial veracity of the record (it may of course have received additions from the reporter, but the part which specially concerns us is not that which would have been interpolated at a later time), we should still be obliged to receive it as an important testimony to the opinion which was entertained in Antioch respecting that which was most characteristic in the belief of Ignatius. Its value Simplicity of Ignatius. consists in this, that Ignatius was not a philosopher, that he had apparently no communication with philosophers, that he was acquainted with scarcely any book but the Jewish Scriptures, that he resorted to them, not for the sake of any deep lore, but to find warnings and examples for the time in which he lived, of the dangers to which they were exposed from envy, ambition, self-will, and of the way in which they might escape those perils. Whatever be our judgment respecting his epistles, our conclusion upon this point will be the same. They stand out in the most marked contrast to the later apologetic literature: they are simple, child-like, practical in the highest degree. The dialogue with Trajan, therefore, must be taken for what it appears on the face of it to be—first, as the expression What his of the simplest conviction of an aged Christian confessor looking testimony death in the face; secondly, as marking out the point of differ- signified. ence which this confessor supposed to exist between him and the heathen people around him; thirdly, as explaining the deepest and most radical ground of the punishment with which the Emperor visited him. He believed that the King and Lord of the whole earth did, in the strictest sense, dwell in him; he believed that the heathen world were doing homage to evil powers, instead of to a perfectly good Being; he believed that he was to proclaim Him who dwelt in him and ruled over him to all men; he believed that, when they acknowledged Him, they would be delivered from their servitude to evil. That there was such a Guide of the wise, the most thoughtful of them had confessed. Even Trajan, in his military Roman manner, claimed for himself a certain belief in such a Director. But Why it Ignatius affirmed that the Invisible Guide had actually come necessarily led to his upon earth, had borne a human nature, had died a human death; condemnation. He was not a mere dæmon, not a special teacher of the wise man —He was the Governor and Ruler of men. To all races and all classes, Syrians and Romans, masters and serfs, His kingdom must be announced. Trajan perceived at once that such a doctrine had nothing of the quietness and harmlessness of a school

dogma. Whatever affinity it might have to the teaching of any Greek or Roman sage, it went altogether beyond the limits within which opinions might be safely tolerated; it united the perils of the definite and the indefinite; it carried you to a depth which no plummet-line could sound,—yet it bore directly upon the common life and common relations of man. If we fairly put ourselves into Trajan's position, we shall certainly not be inclined to condemn his act as a strange or monstrous one. It was that which, in his circumstances, the most tolerant modern statesman might have adopted, if his toleration did not rest upon that belief of a divine guide to Truth which Ignatius proclaimed.

10. Not long after the death of Ignatius, there appeared in the Church of Antioch a man named Saturninus. He is memorable in history as the author of one of the so-called gnostical heresies. We shall not attempt a definition either of the adjective, gnostical, or the substantive, heresy, till we have considered some of the particular appearances from which the names were generalised. The ordinary assertion that Saturninus attempted to connect Christian theology with Persian philosophy, is undoubtedly true; but no power in the world can succeed in connecting two things which have not some natural affinity. The Persian philosophy was nothing except an attempt to inquire into certain puzzling facts which present themselves to the minds of human beings, and which demand a solution. The Christian theology did encounter those facts; they were presumed in it. The single-hearted Ignatius believed that there were powers of evil which were seeking to bring man's spirit into captivity; that the idolatry into which men had fallen, the worship of this visible world, was the effect of the seduction of these evil powers; that there was a Deliverer of man's spirit, One who dwelt with him, and in whom he was to trust. The Persian recognised evil powers; the Persian recognised a power which could overcome them, and which man might obey. He had suspected that the visible world was especially the domain —perhaps the creation—of Ahriman; that Ormuzd belonged to a secret region of light; that he is to be apprehended by some higher faculty. This distinction between mere animal perception and the intuition, or higher knowledge, was not as clear to his mind as it was to that of the Greek, for he had not the same capacity for delicate and accurate distinctions; but it was implied in his belief. No one could doubt that evil things, however secret might be the origin of them, appealed very directly to the senses, are tangible, visible, audible. Only the good man seemed to have a perception of what was

The Syrian Gnosis.

Its relation with Persian faith and philosophy.

The good and evil creators.

THE CHRISTIAN THEOLOGY. 27

beyond these. Surely he must perceive something that was not tangible, visible, audible; surely his perception must have some affinity with goodness. Was this all that the Christian disciple had been taught?—No; he had heard that a spiritual world, a spiritual kingdom, had been unfolded to man. Was he not to explore that spiritual world? Was not the knowledge of it his highest privilege and blessing? Had not St. Paul told him so?

11. But where can be the limit to this knowledge? Who has a right to confine the exercises of the faculty by which it is obtained? It seemed, probably, to Saturninus that the Christian Church had diminished the range of objects which the Persian philosophy had embraced. In the Zendavesta a number of good principles were invoked: Zoroaster seemed to suppose that many powers might have come forth from the source of Good as deliverers from the Evil. Was a new revelation to contract this multitude? Must it not rather make some addition to it? Why should not He of whom the Church spoke have come forth as one, perhaps the last, the highest, of these deliverers, to break the chains of the outward world, the evil kingdom, and shed light into the midst of its darkness? *The Christian intuitions respecting the invisible world.*

12. It was impossible to stop at this point. The Gnostic, however disposed he might be to enlarge the spiritual realm and to discover new forms in it, could not tolerate the notion that any one who had proceeded from it was actually connected with the evil which is inseparable from Matter; He could but have taken the appearance of a mortal body, He could but have undergone an apparent death. Such in its outlines was this early form of Syriac philosophized Christianity. *Docetism.*

13. It was evident that such a faith would provoke no hostility of emperors. If the doctrine was expansive, it was also safe; for what was there in such a scheme which could be the bond of a society, which could make that society suspicious to the Roman state? A theory of the spiritual world might be permitted to any one; the elements of which it consisted might all be furnished by undoubted perceptions of the human spirit; names denoting virtues and principles which men had felt to be precious and real might compose the new economy. But each fresh traveller would suggest a new arrangement of its provinces. The theory of visible and material evil was a perpetual barrier and protection against its intruding into the sphere of practical life. Above all, what centre was there, at once divine and human, to scare the Cæsar on his throne, and to claim a dominion more extensive and permanent than his? *Gnosticism not dangerous to the empire.*

14. Here was the real test. The new revelation was not a

28 GNOSTICISM INVOLVES THE GROWTH OF SECTS.

It can form no society: must lead to infinite sects. revelation of a society for all kindreds and races, if this was the nature and form of it. The Gnosis would take its colour from every different locality, from every different thinker. There must be a Syrian Gnosis and an Alexandrian Gnosis,—one of which the elements were chiefly Jewish, one of which the elements were chiefly Gentile. Basilides, Hermogenes, Valentinus, Carpocrates, a hundred more, each must exhibit his own skill in combination, his skill in tracing the generations of powers and principles, his capacity for spiritual architecture. Each of these men did exhibit talents of no vulgar order; their thoughts, however wild and monstrous they may seem when they are presented together in a system, had each a meaning. Ever and anon one can trace hints of relations between moral qualities which are suggestive, evident tokens that the theorist had seen something of the world he professed to describe, and had brought back a flower from its surface, or a gem out of its recesses. But the members of the different Churches said with emphasis, "You are founders of heresies or sects; you are not adding to our treasures, but robbing us of those we have already. Good news has been preached to man, and you have none for man. A centre has been proclaimed, and you say it does not exist. We felt we had a common fellowship; you substitute a set of notions which are sources of endless division. Lastly, you rob us of all sound morality; you

Perils to morality in Gnosticism. would have us despise our bodies, therefore we cannot keep them pure; you would have us regard the world as necessarily evil, therefore we cannot reform it; you may be ascetics to-day, grossly sensual to-morrow. Each extreme may be defended by the same maxim. A Gnostic is no doubt he that knows, and, therefore, whose life is wholly intellectual, not animal: the Gnostic may become the most animal of all creatures; for why should such a contemptible thing as the flesh not be suffered to sink to the very lowest level which it can reach?"

Mutual dislike of Christians and the philosophical schools connected with Gnosticism. 15. The name of Gnostic became for a long time specially odious in the ears of all members of the Church who did not join one of the Gnostical parties. It was supposed that the most gross of all the heretical schools—that of Carpocrates—held the name by a more pre-eminent title than the rest. The intuition which the doctors of all the schools claimed was opposed on one side to Faith, on another to Action. And as the acknowledgment of this intuition was the bond between the Gnostics within and the philosophers without the Church, the latter began to be more and more suspected as enemies of the Gospel. They frequently justified the charge. The new kingdom evidently interfered with them far more than the old religions were ever likely to do. Questioning seemed at an end if the

Christian dogmatism was to prevail. Philosophical distinctions were extinguished by a message to the ignorant and the evil. The rise of the class of men called Apologists tended to strengthen this mutual animosity. They were polemics by profession, bound to make out a case against their popular as well as their learned antagonists. It was a kind of necessity that they should exhibit that which they were defending in the most definite and tangible form. In arguing with Jews, they of course appealed to the Scriptures; in arguing with Romans, they tried to prove that their faith led to practical moral results. When they met Greeks they might enter more into speculation; but they were always disposed to confute the schools by showing that they had hold of something fixed and positive. *The Apologists.*

16. The earliest Greek apologist who is preserved to us illustrates this tendency in a very remarkable manner. Justin was born in a village of Samaria. He must have conversed much with Jews, though there is no reason to suppose he had any direct affinity with them. He belongs to the crisis of Christian history, when the Church, in consequence of the war in which Barcochba was leader, had become completely separated from the Synagogue. The passages which we shall select from his dialogue with Trypho throw light upon the relation in which Jews as well as Christians of the second century stood to philosophy. *Justin.*

17. If Justin is the hero of his own tale, he was accosted, as he was walking one morning in the portico of a gymnasium, by a man, who hailed him as a philosopher, and presently joined him with several of his friends. When he asks their business, he is told that his companion has learned from a teacher of the Academy always to reverence those who wear the philosophical garb, and, if possible, to make their acquaintance, in hopes of learning something from them. The stranger announces himself as one of the Hebrew race who has been a fugitive after the war. He spent most of his time in Greece, especially at Corinth. Justin asks him what philosophy can help him as much as his law-giver and the prophets? Trypho defends himself by saying that God, His unity, His providence, are the great objects of philosophical investigation. Justin admits this to be the object of philosophy; but he complains that philosophers speak of God as caring for the Universe, for genera and species,—not for individuals, not for you and me. And he does not see how, with such a faith as that, "you and I are to be better or worse." Trypho wishes to know what his own theories are on these matters,—to what school of philosophy he belongs. The question introduces a narrative. Justin fully believes philosophy to be a very great blessing, and one most honoured by God; and *His dialogue with Trypho. The Jew seeking Greek wisdom. Knowledge of God the object of philosophy.*

Justin.

that those are, in the truest sense, holy who have given their mind to it: but he does not believe that any of the sects know what philosophy is, or for what reason it was sent to men. "Knowledge," he says, "is one, but these opinions are various." He had tried most of them. He began with the Stoics: of them he could learn nothing concerning God,—that was not the subject with which they specially occupied themselves. A Peripatetic, to whom he next applied, a sharp clear-sighted man, disgusted him by insisting on a rate of payment for the lectures he gave:—no profit could be expected till that point was settled. An eminent Pythagorean insisted upon such a long preparation in music, astronomy, and geometry, before he could give him any information upon the questions on which he was longing for light, that he left him in despair. He stayed much longer with a Platonist, "for the apprehension of incorporeal things delighted me greatly, and the beholding of ideas gave wings to my intellect, and I thought I had become wise in an incredibly little time, and I hoped that I should presently have the vision of God, for this I knew to be the end of the Platonic philosophy." Then he tells how, when, for the purpose of converse with himself, he had retired to a place not far from the sea, an old man of gentle and venerable appearance entered into discourse with him, and declared himself a Christian. The passages of the discourse which most concern us are these:—"How," said he, "can the philosophers think rightly concerning God, or speak anything truly of Him, not having the knowledge of Him, or having seen Him, or ever heard Him?" "But it is not with the eye," said I, "that the Deity is beheld; with the reason only is it comprehended: so Plato says, and I agree with him." "Are there, then," he said, "in that reason of ours, powers so great and of such a kind; or will the mind of man ever see God, if it hath not been invested with a holy spirit?" "Plato says," said I, "that there is an eye of the mind which is capable of seeing, and which has been given us for the very purpose of seeing purely and undisturbedly that which is. This is the primary and original cause of all that is perceived by the intellect; it hath no form, or colour, or size,—none of those things which the eye takes note of; it is above all substance; it cannot be described or discoursed of; it alone is good and beautiful; it enters into well-constituted souls, in virtue of their relationship to it and their desire to behold it." "What is our relationship," said the old man, "with God? Is it that the soul itself is godly and immortal, and a portion of that royal reason? And when it sees God, is it possible for us to embrace that Divinity which comes in contact with our reason, and thereby to become blessed?" "Cer-

Marginal notes: Trial of the schools. / The new teacher. / Question how the Divinity can be known. / The intellectual and moral insight.

tainly," said I. "Are the same souls," he asked, "in all animals, or is there one soul of a man and one of a horse or an ass?" "The same in all," I answered. "Will, then, horses or asses see, or have they ever seen, God?" "No," said I, "nor will the great majority of men; only he who lives righteously, purifying himself by the exercise of all virtues." "The mind, then, does not see God in consequence of its relationship to Him, nor because it is mind, but because it is temperate and just?" "Yea," said I, "and because it has the capacity of knowing God." "Why, then," said the old man, "do not the animals see God, seeing they have done nothing evil?" "Their body is the hindrance," was the answer.

[margin: Justin. Those who have and have not the capacity to know God.]

The next point discussed between them is the nature of punishment, and how the soul can be better for punishment in another world or condition, if it does not remember what it has been and has done. Thence the old man goes on to proclaim the prophets, who were filled with a true and holy spirit, and not the philosophers, as the true guides to wisdom.

[margin: Punishment and memory.]

The rest of the dialogue is addressed to Trypho's Jewish feelings, and is an argument from the prophets to show that his position is no longer a tenable one.

18. Justin called himself a philosopher, and wore the philosophical cloak to the end of his days. Apparently he held no recognised ecclesiastical office; nevertheless, the simple Ignatius evidently approached more nearly, at certain points, to such a thinker as Plutarch, than he did. The man who knew nothing of what Greek sages had been saying, proclaimed, as part of his baptismal faith, of his Scriptural lore, a conviction which stood in wonderful affinity to some of the thoughts which had been awakened in them; the other, who was conversant with all the terms and methods of the old philosophy, felt a kind of repugnance to it, partly from a conviction of its inadequacy to satisfy his wants, partly from a desire to make the Gospel an antagonist philosophy. The position he took up is a most natural and intelligible one, but it prevented him from doing full justice to those whom he had abandoned,—perhaps from doing full justice to the cause which he had embraced.

[margin: Justin's position.]

19. Justin's first apology was addressed to Antoninus Pius, though it was intended also for his colleague in the empire. His death* is usually, and on good grounds, assigned to the reign of Marcus Aurelius. This Emperor opens a new

[margin: Marcus Aurelius.]

---

* It is commonly ascribed to the intrigues of Crescens, one of the favourite court philosophers. There is no reason to doubt the tradition; the Sophists who basked in the Emperor's patronage seem to have been as despicable as he was noble. That they should have availed themselves of his dislike to the Christians to put down one who adopted their own character, is most natural.

page in our history. Like Plutarch, the Greek and Roman characters were in him remarkably blended; but, unlike Plutarch, the foundation of his mind was Roman: he was a student, that he might more effectually carry on the business of an Emperor. He was therefore not, like Plutarch, first of all a follower of Plato, but, like Seneca and Epictetus, a Stoic. Seneca we mention, however, much more for the sake of their contrast than their resemblance: they were both busy about a practical object, but Marcus Aurelius did not make *his* object the acquisition of personal ease and quietness. He far more resembled Epictetus in the character of his Stoicism: to him he confessed great obligations. But their ends were different, as their positions were different: the slave inquired after the secret of moral freedom; the Cæsar inquired after the secret of Self-government.

20. It would not be easy to find any man in any period of the world's history who pursued this end more strenuously. A Stoic was, in the judgment of Marcus, simply a man who sought carefully and deliberately for the means of ruling himself; he thought it, therefore, not a dereliction of his sect, but a fulfilment of its primary function, if he asked help from every other quarter, as well as from the teachers of the Porch. He opens his first book with an enumeration—a little too formal and elaborate, perhaps, but exhibiting evident and sincere gratitude —of his different benefactors. His mother stands almost first among them; to her he owes his reverence for that which is divine,—a disposition to communicate, a restraint not only upon his actions, but upon his thoughts. He thanks Rusticus for keeping him from the love of sophistry, of rhetoric, of poetry, of all display, whether in speech or in appearance. He thanks Alexander, the Platonist, for teaching him not often, or without necessity, to say to any one, or to write in a letter, that he is busy. From his brother Severus he learned love of justice, love of truth, love of kinsfolk; he learned through him to be acquainted with Cato, Dion, and Brutus, and to conceive of a just polity ordered according to maxims of equality and freedom, and of a kingdom that honours above all things the liberty of the governed. These examples we take at random. The other obligations which he confesses are even more directly for lessons of self-government. The gods he thanks for all kinds of benefits, but especially for good ancestors, good parents, a good sister, good teachers, good members of his household, good kinsmen, good friends. To them, also, he owes it that he had a passion for philosophy, that he did not fall into the hands of any sophist, that he did not waste his time among writers of books, or in unravelling syllogisms, or in studying meteorology.

THE DÆMON WITHIN. 33

19. These indications will, perhaps, suffice to show that the His Roman root of the Emperor's mind was to be found in the old Roman sympathies. discipline of affections and relationships; but that he grafted upon this an amount of self-consciousness and reflection which belong much more to the country whose language he used, than to that of which he was a citizen and ruler. "Every hour think strongly with thyself," he says, " that thou art, as a Roman and as a male, to do that which is before thee with accurate, severe, and unfeigned gravity, with kindliness, and freedom, and justice. And take care to give thyself rest from all surrounding fantasies that may interfere with thy immediate work. And this you will secure if you work each action as if it were Care to the last of your life, avoiding all precipitation and every influ- avoid ence that would withdraw you from the word that has hold of distractions. you (ἀπὸ τοῦ αἱροῦντος λόγου): avoiding also hypocrisy, self-love, discontent with the things that are appointed for you. You see how few the things are, by laying hold of which, a man may live a tranquil and god-conformed life; nor will the gods ask anything more from the man who is careful of these things." Book 2, " Nothing is more miserable," he says in another place, " than chap. 5. the man who is always moving round and round, and surveying all things that lie about him, and prying into the things below the earth and speculating upon that which passes in the souls of his neighbours, and not perceiving that it suffices to dwell with the dæmon within himself, and to serve him manfully. But the service of him is the keeping oneself free from passion Service of and temerity, and from discontent with the things that come within. to us from the gods and from men. For the things that come from the gods are venerable; those from men are dear because of our relationship to them. Some things there are, no doubt, which are sad, in consequence of our ignorance of what is good and what is evil: this blindness is not less than the one which deprives us of the power of distinguishing white and black." Discipline " You must accustom yourself," he says, " only to set such thoughts. images before yourself, that if any one should suddenly ask you, Book 2, what you are now thinking about, you should be able to answer chap. 13. him immediately, with all confidence, *this* or *that;* so that it may be clear at once that all is simple and gracious, and becoming a creature that has fellowship with other creatures, and is indifferent to mere pleasures of sense, and generally to all images of mere enjoyment; and has not rivalry, or envy, or suspicion, or ought else in the mind at which you would blush if you were discovered in it." " Let the god that is in Book 3, thee," he says, shortly after, " be the guardian of a creature chap. 4. that hath the qualities of a male and an elder, and of a political being, and of a Roman, and of a ruler, one that hath set himself

D

in order, one who is awaiting the summons out of life, ready to be set free; one that needeth not an oath, nor any human witness."

The body, soul, and reason. Book 3, chap. 5.

20. The following passage contains something more of formal philosophy, yet combined, as always with practice and self-examination. "Body, soul, reason,—to the body belong sensations, to the soul impulses, to the mind or reason determinations (δόγματα). To receive impressions from outward appearances belongs even to cattle; nervous impulses may belong to wild beasts, to Phalaris, to Nero; to have the reason as a guide in reference to the phenomena that present themselves, may belong to those who do not believe in the gods, and to those who desert their country, and to those who do acts which require that they should shut their doors. If, then, all else is common to these we have enumerated, that which remains as the special gift of the good man is the being content with and welcoming the things that befal him, and those things that have been spun by the destinies for him; the not mixing or disturbing the dæmon that is established in the heart with a crowd of phantasies, but the keeping him propitious, reverently submitting to him, speaking nothing that is contrary to the truth, doing nothing that is beyond the right. And though all disbelieve that such a man is living a simple, and reverend, and brave life, he is not angry with any of them, nor does he turn out of the way that is leading him to the goal of his life, to which he must come pure, silent, ready for dismissal, cheerfully fitted for that which is appointed him."

What distinguishes the good man.

Book 3, chap. 16.

Impressions; how to govern them.

Book 5, chap. 16.

21. Marcus Aurelius had a very strong feeling, like Epictetus, that the management of the impressions which objects make upon us was the chief part of mental discipline. Hear how he applies this to his own position, which was so different from that of Epictetus:—"According to the impressions which thou art continually receiving, will be the temper of thy mind; for the soul gets its dye from these impressions. Dye it then with the continual repetition of such impressions as these: that wheresoever it is appointed you to live, there it is possible to live well; that it is your appointed lot to live in a palace, then it is possible to live well in a palace. And again, that each thing is carried on towards that for the sake of which it has been prepared and ordained. That in that point to which it is bearing, you will find the end or purpose of it; that wherever is the end and purpose of it, there is the good of it; that the good of the reasonable creature is society. That we were born for society, has been shown long ago. For is it not evident that the worse things exist for the sake of the better, the better for the sake of each other? But creatures that have

Social life; its dignity.

life are better than creatures without life, and creatures that have reason are better than those that have merely life."

22. This idea of man as a social or political being enters very deeply into the mind and philosophy of Marcus Aurelius. "We are portions of the great whole" is a thought which continually recurs to him. At times it gives a coldness to his speculations; the man seems in danger of being lost in the universe. But quite as often it is urged as an argument, apparently an effective one to the writer's mind, against selfishness and self-exaltation. Unquestionably he was more inclined than Epictetus was to follow the old Stoics in identifying God with the world—the world signifying not the earth or the visible frame-work of things, but the order and constitution to which we belong. There was much, however, in his Roman education, his devout temper, his personal affections, and his watchfulness over himself, to counteract this tendency. He has no idea of the universe as self-governed. The phrase "directing reason," is one which occurs continually in connection with his idea of the whole; and to this "directing reason" he assigns gracious and human qualities. "The being of the universe," he says, in the beginning of his 6th Book, "is easy to be entreated, and flexible. The reason that directs it hath in itself no motive to ill-doing. Malice is not in it, nor is anything done by it maliciously, nor is anything injured by it. All things come to pass and are accomplished in obedience to it." The first clause of this sentence may seem somewhat unintelligible. The Emperor designs, we apprehend, to oppose the universal substance to that which is the cause of all untractableness, the feelings and passions of the individual. He would lead the man out of these by bringing him to feel that he is not a separate existence, but part of a scheme from which he cannot tear himself without destroying himself. "All particular things," he says just after, "fulfil their end according to the nature of the whole; not in conformity with some other nature, either inclosing it from without, or comprehended within, or existing apart from it and only accidentally attached to it. Either there is in this universe only a mixture of elements, a strange entanglement, to terminate in dispersion and dissolution, or there is unity, order, providence. Supposing the first to be the right view, why do I desire to meddle with such a ferment and confusion of accidents? What else have I to trouble myself about than the how and when I am to become earth? And in that case why do I fret myself? The dissolution will come to me whatever I do. But if the other is the case, I bow down with reverence, I set myself in order, I put confidence in the Director of all things." One extract more may set this point

Tendency to Pantheism; how resisted.

The personality of the divinity he worshipped.

The alternative.

Consequence of either.

Book 6, cc. 9, 10.

36   MARCUS AURELIUS AND THE CHURCH.

clearer:—" All things are woven into one another, and it is a holy combination, and scarcely any two things are heterogeneous. For they have been put together, and together compose the same harmony (συγκοσμἔι τὸν αυτὸν κόσμον). For there is one harmony made up of all things, and there is one God through all things, and one substance and one law, one word or reason that is common to all reasonable creatures, and one truth; since there is also one perfection for all creatures of the same kind, participant of that same word or reason."

Book 7, chap. 9.

23. This last sentence will so immediately recall to the reader's mind one of St. Paul's, that the question naturally suggests itself,—What is the relation between them? How was Marcus Aurelius likely to regard those who held the faith of St. Paul? How did he actually regard them? On the last point there is no doubt. The Church had far more to suffer from Marcus, than from his son Commodus; he deliberately adopted the policy which Trajan had originated, he followed it out with far greater severity than Trajan. All the arguments which recommended it to the one Emperor, presented themselves with new force to his successor; they were strengthened by considerations peculiar to himself. As Marcus Aurelius was more devout than his predecessors, as the worship of the gods was with him less a mere deference to opinion and tradition, he felt a more hearty indignation against those who seemed to be undermining it. As he had more zeal for the well-being of his subjects, and a stronger impression of the danger of their losing any portion of the faith and reverence which they had, the political motives which swayed earlier emperors acted more mightily upon him. As he had convinced himself that the severest course of self-discipline is necessary in order to fit a man for overcoming the allurements of the visible and the terrors of the invisible world, he despised and disbelieved those who seemed to have attained the results without the preparatory processes. As he wished to reconcile the obligations of an emperor to perform all external duties with the obligation of a philosopher to self-culture, and found the task laborious enough, the strange mixture of the ideas of a polity with ideas belonging to the spiritual nature of man, which he heard of among the Christians, must have made him suspect them of aping the Cæsars and the Roman wisdom in their government, as well as of aping the Stoics in their contempt of pain. Such reasons, if we made no allowance for the malignant reports of courtiers and philosophers, the prevalent belief of unheard-of crimes in the secret assemblies of the Christians, the foolish statements and wrong acts of which they may themselves have been guilty, will explain sufficiently why the venerable age and character of Polycarp, the beautiful fidelity

Relation of Marcus Aurelius to the Christian Church.

Causes of his dislike,

political, religious, philosophical.

of the martyrs of Lyons, did not prevent them from being victims of the decrees of the best man who ever reigned in Rome.

24. Any notion, therefore, that the great principles and maxims which are announced in the writings of Marcus Aurelius were derived from Christian teachers, or indicated even a partial allegiance to Christian maxims, must be at once discarded, not merely as wanting evidence, but as refuted by it. *Affinity of his doctrines with Christian doctrines: how accounted for.* The question, what relation there is between his principles and those which the teachers of the Gospel were promulgating, is a very different one, and cannot be resolved by any hasty inferences from the treatment which they received at his hands. Those who think of the Christian Church as a mere human society set up in the world to defend a certain religion against a certain other religion, will naturally try to prove that its members were in possession of truth by proving that its opponents were only asserters of falsehood. Those who believe that it was a society established by God as a witness of the true constitution for all human beings, will rejoice to acknowledge its members to be what they believed themselves to be—confessors and martyrs for a truth which they could not embrace or comprehend, of which they often perceived only a small portion, but which, through their lives and deaths, as well as through the right and wrong acts, the true and false words, of those who understood them least, was to manifest and prove itself. *The human and divine solution.* Those who hold this conviction dare not conceal, or misrepresent, or undervalue, any one of those weighty and memorable sentences which are to be found in the meditations of Marcus Aurelius. If they did, they would be undervaluing a portion of that very truth which the preachers of the Gospel were appointed to set forth; they would be adopting the error of the philosophical emperor without his excuses for it. Nor dare they pretend that, by some means or other, the Christian preaching had unconsciously imparted to him a portion of its own light even while he seemed to exclude it. They will believe that it was God's good pleasure that a certain great truth should be seized and apprehended by this age, and they will see indications of what that truth was in the efforts of Plutarch to understand the dæmon which guided Socrates, in the courageous language of the Martyr of Antioch, in the bewildering dreams of the Gnostics, in the eagerness of Justin to prove Christianity a philosophy, and to confute the philosophers, in the apprehension of Christian principles by Marcus Aurelius, and in his hatred of the Christians. From every side they will derive evidence that a doctrine and society which are meant for mankind, cannot depend upon the partial views and apprehensions of men, but must go on justifying, reconciling, confuting those views and apprehensions by the demonstration of facts.

CHAPTER II.

THE THIRD CENTURY.

FROM MARCUS AURELIUS TO CONSTANTINE.

The Emperors after Marcus; their common object.
1. THE miserable period from the death of Marcus Aurelius to the accession of Septimius Severus, explains the difference between the characteristics of the 2d and of the 3d centuries. The effort to make despotism orderly and righteous, to give an empire the form of a republic, had been continued with different degrees of earnestness, ability, and success, through four reigns; the climax of the experiment was in the last. The Roman world saw that it had failed. Something was wanting besides the honesty, self-restraint, philosophy, of the temporary ruler. All these qualities, combined with a resolute purpose of crushing what seemed hostile to the integrity of the empire, and the belief of the people in its divine protectors, had given the Roman world an appearance of stability which the accession of one contemptible ruffian could at once turn into a mockery. The meaning of the word Imperator, the basis on which the imperial power was standing, the instruments which must overthrow it, then made themselves evident to all tolerably thoughtful observers. The question, how the dissolution of the Society might be for the longest time averted, became the only one which an intelligent ruler had to propose to himself. Various answers were found for it during the 3rd century. Strive to preserve the traditional reverence for Roman law, so you may at least impose some restraint upon the power of arms, was the suggestion which the sage juris-

Policy of S. Severus,
consults of the first Severus offered to him, and upon which he endeavoured to act. An eclectical unity, resulting from a tolerance and comprehension of different parties, seems to have

Of Alex. Severus and Philippus,
been dreamed of by Alexander Severus, and to have been carried out with more of ambition and vanity by Philippus Arabs.

Of Decius,
Stern discipline, and consequent restraint upon all novelties of opinion, appeared to Decius, who saw the weakness of this last attempt, the only remedy for the mischiefs to which it had led. To divide the empire under different heads, and to give it more the character of an oriental government, was the policy of

Diocletian. These are the only distinct purposes which presented themselves in that age. The rest of the Emperors chose one or other of them, or merely yielded to their passions, not setting before themselves any end at all. *Of Diocletian.*

2. The preservation or pursuit of unity therefore marks and defines this period much more distinctly than the last. What is true of the statesmen, is equally true of the philosophers. Each experiment in the world had one which corresponded to it in the schools, as well as in the hearts of human beings. The 3rd century is eminently a philosophical century, for it is one in which the great problem of philosophy forced itself upon men's minds, from whatever point they might start, into whatever lines of thought they might diverge. The ultimate ground of unity, as well as the conditions under which men might actually become one, alike engaged the thoughts of the soldier, the lawyer, the solitary thinker, of the doctor and the disciple, of the persecutor and the martyr. *How the world and the schools answer to each other.*

3. In spite of the strong opposition which began to display itself during the 2d century between the Christian preachers and the Pagan philosophers, we have seen that there were tendencies to approximation between them, and that the violent efforts of the Gnostics to pour the new wine into the old bottles, had been one main occasion of their repugnance. In the latter part of that century, some feeling of the connexion began to manifest itself on the other side. If we had not heard of Philo, we might be disposed to wonder that the Judaical element in Christianity should be that which most attracted the notice and sympathy of a Pagan speculator. This appears to have been the case with Numenius. We are bound to speak with hesitation about him, because we derive our knowledge of him from the work of Eusebius, on the Preparation for the Gospel, a work written with a special purpose, and by a man with a strong Alexandrian bias. Still we have no reason to suspect the Church historian of quoting unfaithfully, and it is from his extracts, not from his comments, that we may form our conclusions. The most important sentiment which is attributed to Numenius, we have on the earlier and higher authority of Clemens. " Numenius, the Pythagorean philosopher," he says, " plainly writes, what is Plato but Moses talking Attic?" Clemens apparently supposed Numenius to hint at some historical relation between them, for in the same paragraph he quotes Jewish authors, who held the Greek philosophers, as they naturally would, to be copiers of their books, or inheritors of their traditions. Numenius may have indulged in guesses as random and uncertain as those of Clemens, or of the Jews, upon this subject; but his feeling *Numenius the Pythagorean.* *Notion of a union between Jewish and Gentile wisdom.* *Præp. Evang. Book 9, cc. 7, 8.*

40 THE ABSOLUTE GOD.

respecting the moral relation between Plato and Moses is not in the least affected by them. Plato is certainly *not* Moses talking Attic. No two great men were ever more unlike in the habit of their thoughts, or in the work which they had to do. But it is very important for the history of this period, to know that there were men, reflecting and earnest men, who were unable to perceive this difference, and who did perceive an agreement between the two minds, which they could only express to themselves in some phrase like that which we have quoted. It is one of the signs of the craving for reconciliation which was working in various directions, a craving which led then, as it leads always, to a number of practical as well as theoretical confusions, but which was pointing to deep principles concerning the life of Man and the nature of God.

The opinion of their similarity, instructive.

4. The ground of the similarity which Numenius discovered between Plato and Moses, is evident from an extract which Eusebius gives from his book concerning the Good. " The Being," he says, " is fixed and eternal, ever the same in itself, and in the same, hath never perished, or increased or decreased, is susceptible of no accidents, or movements, or locality." Here, no doubt, he found the beginning and real object of the Platonical search. The well-known passages which Eusebius quotes from the Hebrew Scriptures, " I am the Lord who change not;" " They shall perish, but Thou art the same, and Thy years shall not fail;" might well strike the Pythagorean as wonderful anticipations of Greek discoveries. Probably he was much more impressed by observing that these were not isolated passages, but stood in the most intimate relation with the whole record in which they occurred. At the same time, the historical character of that record might be easily forgotten or overlooked by one who was in search of principles rather than of facts. The other greater distinction which was involved in this, that in Moses the Being is speaking, acting, declaring Himself, may not have been unobserved by Numenius; but he may have thought that this was implied, if not expressed, in the creed and enquiries of Plato, and he may have felt that for his own age it was quite necessary that the omission, if it was one, in the thoughts of the Greek, should be supplied, that in some way or other the absolute ground of all things should be confessed as a person, and should enter into communication with his creatures.

Præp. Evang. book 11, chap. 10.

5. How this could be he seems to have undertaken to explain in a very memorable passage which occurs in the 11th book of Eusebius, out of all chronological order, as it follows a long extract from Plotinus. The passage is written with great caution and reverence. Numenius begins with a prayer that

Awfulness of the inquiry. The secondary god. Præp. Evang. book 3, c.18.

THE GOD IN COMMUNICATION WITH MATTER. 41

God himself may be the standard and rule of his utterances, that He will open to him the treasury of thought, since he is convinced that whoever snatches at it eagerly and irreverently will find it turn to ashes. Then he proceeds, " That primary or Highest God being in himself, is altogether simple, conversing altogether with himself, nowise to be divided. But the god who is the second and third is one. Moving about, however, in matter which is dual, he unites it and yet is divided by it; seeing that it is fluxional, and hath a certain appetitive character. Therefore, not being in direct communication with the purely noetic—for so he would be wholly occupied with himself—by looking upon matter, he becomes occupied with that, and as it were unobservant of himself. And he touches and deals with that which is sensible, and draws it up into his own proper character, stretching himself out to (or with a view to stretch himself out so as to take up) the material." He goes on a little after to distinguish between the primary God and the Demiurgus or Creator. The first must be looked upon as the father of the second, for of Him, the primary Being, it would be impious to predicate any activity. "The primary God," he says, " must be free from all works, and a king. But the Demiurgus must exercise government, going through the heavens. Through him comes this our condition; through him Reason being sent down in transit or efflux (ἐν διέξοδῳ) to hold communion with all that are prepared for it. God then looking down and turning himself to each of us, it comes to pass that our bodies live and are nourished, receiving strength from the outer rays that come from Him. But when God turns us to the contemplation of Himself, it comes to pass that these things are worn out and consumed, but that the reason lives, being made partaker of a blessed life." *The great Paradox.*

The Demiurgus.

The divinely communicated Mind or Reason.

6. The introduction to this passage is not less important than the doctrine which it contains. Serious men evidently began to tremble when they perceived into what awful depths they were plunging. They felt that there was no shrinking even from such questions as those which Numenius grapples with here: some secret necessity was enforcing the study of them: philosophy and practical life seemed both to have some strange connection with them. But to enter upon them rashly, with unhallowed unprepared hearts, how infinitely perilous this must be! how certainly the conscience and moral being of the intruder into the sanctuary must suffer, even if he was not permitted to deface or to destroy any of its treasures! It is difficult to measure the extent of this feeling in the 3d century. Some of the truest and some of the falsest tendencies in the Schools as in the Church had their origin in it. A Pythagorean *The secret discipline.*

42   THE LATIN AND GREEK CITIES.

like Numenius was sure to feel with especial strength the duty of meditating in silence upon principles lying so near to the heart of man, and yet so far beyond his conceptions. He, of all persons, would be most likely to teach that only a band of carefully disciplined scholars should hear these topics broached, or be tempted to investigate them. No one seems to have felt more strongly than Numenius, how much the different philosophies had lost their relation to each other, as well as their internal meaning, in their transmission through different generations of expositors and disputants. His history of the Platonic school, part of which is preserved by Eusebius, seems to have been written for the purpose of establishing this point, and of reclaiming Plato for a true guide into those mysteries to which the Samian teacher had pointed the way ;—a worthy and noble object, yet one which would almost inevitably give birth to a kind of pride, different in form, but not in principle, from that which it displaced.

The profaneness of the schools.

7. Numenius was a Syrian. But we must turn to two other portions of the Roman world before we can understand how thoughts like his were likely to work, and what different fruits they would produce, according to the minds with which they came in contact. No countries ever presented so remarkable a moral and intellectual contrast to each other as the African province of which Carthage was the capital, and Egypt, as represented in the city of the Ptolemies. Both these countries (of course we do not refer to the rural districts in either) had attained a high refinement and civilization. But the civilization of the one was of the most strictly Latin, the other of the most strictly Greek type. The victory of Rome over its ancient rival was very imperfectly exhibited in the conquests of either Scipio. The subsequent transformation of the whole Punic mind, under the influence of Roman institutions and education, was infinitely more wonderful. In Carthage we may see the simple and naked effects of Roman discipline, not counteracted nor modified by those strange elements which it met with among the Gothic or Gothicized nations of modern Europe. Legal and rhetorical forms had there their full sway over the mind. In the school, almost in the nursery, the habits of the advocate and the jurist were forming themselves, and giving the impulse and direction to all the activity and vehemence of the African character. In Carthage, as in all the great cities of the Empire, the Christian Church found a home. Before the end of the 2d century, eminent writers had appeared among its members. The most illustrious of them suggests some curious topics of reflection to the historian of philosophy. No man could detest it more cordially than Tertullian. Plato and

Carthage and Alexandria.

Tertullian.

Aristotle were in his judgment the sources of every detestable doctrine which had obtained currency among the heretics of the Church. "What communion," he asked, "could there be between the synagogue and the porch? How was it possible that men who had inherited a divine doctrine should turn again to be seekers and enquirers?" In vain it was suggested to him that the words "Ask and ye shall receive, seek and ye shall find," had proceeded from the highest of all authorities; he peremptorily decided that that sentence was only intended for those who had not yet learnt the doctrine of the Church, and was utterly inapplicable to any who had. No one ever possessed a more remarkable facility of appealing to authority for the purpose of silencing argument, or of flying to argument for the purpose of evading authority. Though he feared to be indebted to Greek sages, he had not the least fear of incurring obligations to Roman lawyers. The maxim of the courts, that a certain term of uninterrupted possession is a bar to any adverse claim, was at once transferred by him to spiritual treasures; a plea which was good for the defence of houses and lands, must be good for the defence of moral and divine principles. Always alive to the perils of the student, of which he knew almost nothing, he never seems to have anticipated the least danger from the temptations of the rhetorician, or of a fierce African temper, both of which, one would fancy, must have been besetting him every hour. He was ever on the watch against some form of error, yet he never thought it an error—doubted that it was a virtue—to suspect an opponent's motives, or to impute intentions to him of which he may have been innocent. And therefore it seems to have been permitted, by a most righteous dispensation, and for a most useful warning to after times, that the great denouncer of heretics should end by becoming a heretic.

8. It may readily be admitted—we have all along asserted —that there is a most valuable side of truth presented to us in the Roman mind, without which the Greek side would be utterly imperfect. Any one who looks upon the Christian Church as intended to combine and reconcile different habits and modes of feeling apparently opposed, must demand that there should be in it representatives of each of these characters. Were we contemplating Tertullian on his positive side, we should speak gratefully of his fervid eloquence, of the light he has thrown on various truths which Gnostics and Spiritualists have disguised or denied, of the use of his labours in preventing a society of men from becoming a school of doctors, of his services in showing that old legal maxims do contain a moral signification. It is not our duty nor our wish to disparage any

De Præscript. Hæretic. § 7. Ipsæ denique hæreses a Philosophia subornantur, etc. Quid ergo Athenis et Hierosolymis. eod. loc. Quærendum est donec invenias, et credendum ubi inveneris; at nihil amplius nisi custodiendum quod credidisti: § 8.

Merits of Tertullian.

one of his excellencies, nor to deal hardly with defects for which his education and position offer so valid an excuse, and which may, if we please, be salutary, not injurious, to ourselves. But to the historian of Philosophy, he presents himself merely as pugnacious and destructive. We must, in self-defence, sternly resist Tertullian's denunciations, and any canons which he has invented for the purpose of enforcing them. Unless we do so, we must condemn a class of men, contemporaries of Tertullian, his equals in every Christian gift, immeasurably his superiors in the grace of humility, who followed a course as nearly as possible the opposite of his. Nay, every after age, as well as every section of Christendom, is interested in this opposition to Carthaginian dogmas. Luther, and all who have followed him in appealing to a higher and elder law than Tertullian's rule of prescription, are not greater rebels against his authority than Augustine, Anselm, Aquinas. If he was right, their dallying with the questions in which the moralists and metaphysicians of the old world took part,—their reverence for Plato or Aristotle,—must degrade them from doctors to infidels.

Why he must be opposed.

9. The Christian Church in Alexandria had more temptation than any Carthaginian could have had, to protest against the old philosophers, for they had been brought into immediate contact with the dangers which Tertullian contemplated from a distance. Gnosticism, as we have hinted already, had established itself very early among them. For one sect or form of it which appeared in Syria, they might reckon twenty. The relation, too, in which these sects stood to the heathen sects, as well as to the school of Philo, was obvious. It did not require polemical ingenuity to trace the affinity or the descent; the offenders would themselves have acknowledged it and boasted of it. It was most likely that such a discovery should have produced in Alexandrian Christians a dread of all intercourse with living teachers of philosophy, or with the books that contained it. We have no facts which can enable us to refute that supposition, for the history of the Egyptian Church is almost a blank till nearly the end of the 2d century. But this we can affirm confidently, that the moment it ceases to be a blank, when illustrious teachers begin to appear in it, this reactionary tendency has been entirely overcome, and a new course has been commenced, entirely in accordance with the character of the city to which this Church belonged. The Christian doctors of whom we shall have to speak, did not tremble at the name of Philo, but eagerly availed themselves of his wisdom; did not set up Dogmatism against Gnosticism, but affirmed that there was a true Gnosis which was the only effectual antidote of the false; did not repudiate the thoughts and inquiries of former

The Alexandrian characteristic.

Christian motives for dreading Philo.

generations of Greeks, but attributed them to Him from whom the new covenant proceeded, and regarded them as preparations for it.

10. Of Pantænus, the first teacher of this school, there is little to record. The missionary activity which is attributed to him by historians, must have been connected with that belief in a Divine Guide of men, who was educating them through preparatory stages for the highest wisdom, which was afterwards brought out in its clearness and fulness by Clemens. His name is so memorable in connection with the movements of this age, that we must speak of him at some length. And as we have not the good fortune to possess biographical details respecting him, like those which throw so much light upon the writings of his successor Origen, we must confine ourselves to such extracts as seem fittest to explain the purpose of his three principal treatises. The shortest of them, which is especially addressed to Heathens, seems at first sight at variance with the maxims which we have attributed to his school. It evinces certainly a more intense repugnance to idolatry in its outward forms and in its inward nature, than Tertullian can ever have felt. The deliverance of the human spirit from idolatry, and all the moral fruits of it, is that which Clemens regards as the highest blessing which man can receive,—as the great end of the divine counsels respecting him. The legends of the poets are odious to him, because he supposes that they have been ministers of idolatry, though he discovers in them certain adumbrations of divine truths. The music of Orpheus, and Amphion, and Arion, he thinks only tended to excite the passions, and seduce men by a certain enchantment into the worship of visible things; but it bore witness of a higher and more celestial harmony, which has spoken to the heart and spirit, and drawn them away from the objects and appetites to which they naturally become enslaved. The different theories of the philosophers respecting the gods, are not in general spoken of with more respect. The search for elements by the Ionic school struck Clemens as simply materialistic. The resolution of all things into the infinite, as well as the speculations respecting space, terminated, he supposes, naturally in the Atheism of the later schools. It is only when he comes to Plato, that Clemens pauses to express an admiration and sympathy, which are yet by no means rapturous or unqualified.

"I desire," he cries, " not the winds, but the Lord of the winds; not the fire, but the Lord of the fire; not the world, but the Artificer of the world; not the sun, but Him who brings light to the sun; I seek God, not the works of God. Whom shall I have with me, as my fellow-labourer in this enquiry? I

46   THE EXHORTATION TO THE GENTILES.

The search for God. cannot disclaim thee, Plato, if thou wilt go along with me. But tell me, then, Plato, in what way we must trace the footsteps of the God? *It is a mighty work to find the Father and Creator of this great whole. And having found, to speak of Him to all is impossible.* Why so? Because, thou sayest, *He is in no wise expressible in language.* Right, O Plato; thou touchest the truth. But thou shouldest not have despaired. Join me in the search concerning the *good;* for some divine efflux hath descended upon all men whatsoever, especially on those who are occupied about wisdom. Wherefore even unwillingly they confess, that there is one God, indestructible and unbegotten; that he is somewhere behind the heaven, dwelling always in his own proper habitation. 'Tell me,' says Euripides, 'What kind of God we are to conceive of Him that seeth all things, and Himself is unseen.' Menander was therefore evidently bewildered when he said, ' O sun, for thee must we worship as the first of gods, by whose light it is permitted us to see the other gods.' The sun would never shew that true God. He is shewn as by that pure Word who is the Sun of the soul, by whose rising within in the depth of the reason, the eye of the reason itself is illuminated........ Plato indicates Him thus: All things are about the King of all, and He is the author of all that is good."

Having discovered this one memorable exception to the idolatrous tendency of the surrounding world, Clemens proceeds to notice others, both poets and philosophers, who bore at least an unconscious testimony to the invisible God. " Xenophon," he said, " would have spoken openly, if he had not feared his master's hemlock." He repeats the hymn of Cleanthes, alludes to the dogmas of the Pythagoræans, extracts passages even from poets, from Hesiod, Homer, Sophocles, Euripides, and Aratus, affirming the principle which the popular creed denied.

Explanation of this treatise. 11. There is no real contradiction between this treatise and one of which we shall have to speak presently. They belong no doubt to different periods and states of Clemens's mind; but the principle in them is the same, and the growth from one to the other orderly and natural. Clemens recognises a conflict going on unceasingly in the minds of all persons in the old world, consciously in the minds of its most conspicuous teachers, between a power of sense which the greater part obeyed, and a divine teacher whom even in the midst of their slavery they confessed. His business and vocation as a Christian teacher is to proclaim to all this Guide and Illuminator of the heart and conscience, to declare the outward facts by which He has made known His presence and His power, to invite all to embrace His government. The belief of such a divine teacher was in the judgment of Clemens the antidote to that Gnosticism which exalted the intuitions of man so highly, and made them at the same time so precarious and contradictory. The man was not exploring for himself; he was perpetually under guidance. There was not a separate revelation for each man; there was one divine truth, one object, the knowledge of whom was the highest reward that could be granted to any.

12. The difference between Clemens and the pseudo-gnostic, comes out most strikingly in the next treatise, Ο Παιδαγωγος. The whole of this very striking discourse is employed in pointing out the gracious human discipline which the divine teacher uses with men, in order to lead them to that highest knowledge which he designs for them. The practical life which was so divorced from the speculative by the gnostical teachers, is here shown to be its necessary condition. The opening of the book will explain the relation between this treatise and its predecessor, the anthropology of Clemens generally, and the inseparable connexion of that anthropology with his divinity. He describes man as a threefold creature, possessing habits or a certain mould of character, practical or intended for action, susceptible of affections or passions. The Divine Word he speaks of as having a threefold office, corresponding to these distinctions of the creature whom He undertakes to educate. The discipline of the habits or character he would call protreptic, of the actions hypothetic, of the passions paramuthetic. By the first word, he appears to understand the giving a new purpose or inclination to the man; by the second the suggestion of methods for accomplishing the end which he hath set before himself; by the third the purifying imfluences whereby the wounds in the soul are healed, and it is made capable of a higher love. His purpose in this treatise is not to speak of the infusion of a new principle, so much as the cultivation of one which has been already confessed. He proposes to consider the Divine Word rather as a guide in practice than as an instructor in doctrine; to set Him forth as the conductor of a moral rather than of a scientific training. It is not, he intimates, that he in the least undervalues that training, or can attribute it to any less than a divine school-master, but that his immediate object is to contemplate Him in the other aspect.

The divine discipline of the human spirit.

Relation of this discipline to the history of philosophy.

13. The importance of this treatise to the ecclesiastical historian, and to the practical moralist, is, we think, very great. The historian of philosophy has not the same excuse as they have for entering into the details of it. But he would be guilty of a great omission if he passed it over upon the plea that it belongs more to the province of the divine than to his, or that so much of it is occupied with questions of practice rather than speculation. It will have been seen from the extract which we

Relation of this treatise to philosophy.

have given out of Numenius, how much the thoughts of men everywhere were exercised with difficulties respecting a primary absolute Being dwelling in His own perfection, and one who is cognisable by human faculties, though not by the human senses; who holds relations with matter, though for the purpose of raising spirit above matter. This deep enquiry had been suggested to heathen philosophers by the facts of their own lives. It was connected with a long line of previous enquiries, conducted by the most earnest and painful thinkers. Some solution of the difficulty must be found. The demand for unity, the great demand of this time, was seen to be involved in it. The more philosophers sought for unity, the more discontented they were with the reverence for divided objects; the more this duplicity presented itself to them, the more closely it seemed to be involved with the very roots of their own being, with the existence of man, and the foundations of the universe. The attempt of Numenius to find his way out of the difficulty may seem to us in many respects confused and unsuccessful; yet surely no one can consider it without wonder, and some increased insight into the nature of the problem, into its depth, and yet into its practical significance. It seems like entering into a new world to pass from such a speculation to such words as these of Clemens. "This teacher of ours, O my children, is like to His Father, *the* God, of whom He is the sinless Son, having His soul free from all passions, God unpolluted though in human form, the Divine Word, He that is in the Father, He that is on the right hand of the Father, and in His form divine. He is that stainless image which is set before us. Let us strive with all our might to bring our souls to His likeness." Or this: "Naturally therefore is the man dear to God, seeing that he is His handywork. And all things else He only made by commanding them to exist; but the man He wrought by His own hands, and infused into him something that belongs to Himself...... The man, then, whom God hath made is chosen for his own sake. But that which is loved for its own sake is intimately related to Him by whom it is so loved, and that is of all things most heartily welcomed and embraced." The whole education of man being, according to Clemens, grounded in this original love, and being carried on with the most regular method in order to produce the reaction and reciprocation of love in the creature who is the object of it, we have something very different from the view of the Demiurgus, whose connection with matter it was so hard to explain; a very different relation between him and the primary God, with whom Numenius felt he must be united, and yet from whom, that he might converse with matter, he must be separated. The contrast is great, and yet who does not feel that both teachers are occupied with the same mighty problem, and that if Clemens has the glimpse and apprehension of a higher unity than Numenius had, it is in a great measure because he looked at the whole subject in a more practical light, and was able to contemplate the Creator and Archetype of man as actually engaged in renewing His image in him?

14. We wish to point out this relation between a treatise which is not formally philosophical, and the philosophy of the time, before we proceed to the largest work of Clemens, in which he directly addresses himself to the subject of philosophy, and defends himself from the charge of meddling with topics which a Christian teacher would be wiser to pass by. The Stromata, as its name indicates, is a collection of patch-work, each piece of which, Clemens believes, has some duty of its own, and some relation to the others, and which the truly instructed Divine Artificer can bring together, so that they shall form a consistent whole. Seeing that all the treasures of Clemens' past readings were to be laid under contribution for this work, it was needful that he should assert his right to deal with those authors whom Tertullian would have banished altogether from the divine republic. Against those who affirm that philosophy has polluted life, being the artificer of falsehood and foul works, he boldly affirms it to be an evident likeness or image of the truth, a divine gift bestowed upon the Greeks. In studying it, he affirms that he is not carried away by the enchantment of a deceitful art, but that he is engaging in an exercise which is an ally and demonstration of faith. He allows most readily that there is a false philosophy, and that " great is the danger of parading the unspeakable word of the real philosophy before those who desire merely to argue and contradict, who throw about words and names without order or reverence. They who trifle thus," he says, " deceive themselves, and play tricks with all who adhere to them." But in direct opposition to the dogma of Tertullian, about asking and seeking, he affirms that, " as the lover of the chase values the animal which he has pursued long, tracked out, searched for in holes and bye-places, followed with his dogs ; so that truth appears in all its sweetness when it has been hunted for and won by toil." He argues from the law and the prophets, that all forms of wisdom and art are from God. " The wise in mind," he says, " have no doubt some peculiar endowment of nature. But when they have offered themselves for their work, they receive a spirit of perception from the highest Wisdom, giving them a new fitness for it." He insists upon all laborious

E

HIS VIEWS OF GREEK PHILOSOPHY.

Cap. 5, § 32. study, as well as sympathetic feeling, as a proper exercise and cultivation of this spiritual endowment. Having adopted from Philo an ingenious and fantastic Scripture allegory in defence of this proposition, he utters these memorable words. "We affirm then from hence, in plain words, that philosophy carries on an inquiry concerning Truth and the nature of being, and this Truth is that concerning which the Lord Himself said, 'I am the Truth.'.... And when the initiated find or rather receive the true philosophy, they have it from the Truth itself."

Stromata, c. 7, § 37. 15. "It appears to me then," says Clemens, "that that whole discipline of the Greeks, with philosophy itself, came down from God upon men, not according to a distinct pre-ordination, but in the same way as the rains pour themselves forth, both on the good ground and on the dung-heaps, and on the house-tops. On all these grass and corn bud forth, nay sometimes figs and some of the hardier trees spring upon the very tombs. Those sown in the most careless way bend like the truest specimens of their kind, because they have enjoyed the same influence from the rain, but those which have not had the advantage of good ground wither or are plucked up." He applies the parable of the sower in illustration of this position, contends that all plants whatever which are good for life have the same sower and husbandman, as all arts and sciences which are necessary for their cultivation proceed from *§ 30.* the same wisdom. Philosophy, of course, in so large and catholic a view, must take a very high place among God's gifts. "And when I speak of philosophy," says Clemens, "I do not mean the Stoic, or the Platonic, or the Epicurean, or the Aristotelic, but whatsoever hath been said in each of these sects well, teaching righteousness with reverent science. All this I call Philosophy; to this I give the name Eclectic. But whatsoever they have cut out or cut off by their mere human reasonings, these I should never call divine."

16. These patches from Clemens, though they may give little notion of the long and elaborate work from which they are taken, may suffice for the purpose of such a treatise as this. They will at least show what place Clemens holds among the thinkers of the early centuries after Christ. There are two passages, or rather two words, that have occurred in the course of our extracts, to which we would direct the attention of our readers before we part with this author. One is the word *The initiated.* "*initiated*," the other is "*eclectic*." These are great and significant expressions in the history of that time, and of subsequent times. It is very necessary that we should examine into them if we would know anything of the Pagan or of the

HIS IDEA OF AN ESOTERICAL DOCTRINE. 51

Christian philosophy of the 3d century, or of the relation in which they stood to each other.

17. When we are told, as we so often are, by a certain class of commentators on ecclesiastical history, that the Christian teachers derived their notion of a lore which was not to be communicated to the vulgar herd, but to be reserved for those who had passed through certain stages of discipline, from the Pythagorean doctors, a half truth is uttered, which, like all half truths, may lead us into decided falsehood. That this was a time in which the Pythagorean discipline put itself forth with a power which it had scarcely possessed even in the first days of the political community in southern Italy, we might infer from the cases of Apollonius and Numenius, if there were not the additional and still more conclusive evidence of Lucian to establish the opinion. His ridicule had no doubt abundant and most legitimate scope for its exercise in the quacks and mountebanks who practised mystifications, sometimes mischievous, sometimes only foolish, under the name of mysteries, or who made the glories of science the theme of continual prating. Lucian, of course, never took the pains to distinguish these pretenders from the truer men whom they counterfeited. Their real awe and conscientious belief were quite unintelligible to his lively, sparkling, clear-sighted incredulity. But that such men as Numenius trembled, not at the shows and forms of things,—at the masks and phantoms of a degrading demoniacal superstition,—but at the actual presence of a Being whom they adored and wished to love, seems to us unquestionable. Was the Christian a plagiarist if he believed that he was to take his shoes from off his feet when he was admitted into the same presence? What did his faith mean, if he was not admitted into it? And yet could he hide from himself the fact that there were numbers professing that faith, to whom it had no such signification; many entirely wrapt up in material pursuits, who yet had committed no scandals that should exclude them from the fellowship of the Church; many with honest and affectionate hearts desirous of light, and yet who seemed unable to contemplate spiritual objects, except under sensual forms, which contracted, often distorted, them? The nature of the difference which we have pointed out between the belief of Numenius and that of Clemens, did not seem to involve a difference between them in this respect. The divine and philanthropical Teacher, far more than the mere Demiurgus, might desire to proportion the degrees of light which He revealed to the organs which were intended to receive it. The Perfect Love which casts out fear, may demand a reverence greater than it is possible to feel for the mere absolute entity

Was the word borrowed from the Pythagoreans.

Christian excuses for the idea.

which haunted, though it did not satisfy, the reason of the Pythagorean.

Idea of sacrifice.

18. In this sense, then, the Christian who spoke of the " initiated " disciple, used language which seemed even more appropriate to him than it could be to the philosopher. Nor must it be omitted that he had another claim to this mode of speech, and to the thoughts which it expressed. The Pythagoræan had risen above the dark faith in the necessity of propitiations to an evil divinity. Sacrifice was to him little more than a process of purification. The Christian had equally abjured the traditional sacrifices, so far as they implied appeals to any thing which is evil; but he had recognised sacrifice as importing reconciliation and renewed fellowship with a perfectly good Being; not merely an act on the part of the worshipper, but as originating with the object of his worship. Such a sacrifice could not but seem to him in the highest sense a Mystery. In proportion as he was aware of the counterfeit notions which surrounded the idea of sacrifice, and the temptations of uninstructed sensual men to substitute them for it, he would have a motive to insist upon that name, and carefully to guard this sacred truth from the intrusion of profane speculators.

Dangers of the disciplina arcani.

19. Thus the *disciplina arcani* which has been so much spoken of in the early Church, touched at one point upon the philosophical, at the other upon the religious, habits and feelings of the surrounding world. It was not really derived from either. It testified to the fact that the Christian Church had a real relation to both those sides of truth which among heathens had been almost inevitably separated. But it is impossible to deny that there lay in one aspect of this discipline all the temptations to philosophical pride, in the other to religious imposture, which had been at work in the old world. The initiated disciple who was admitted into a higher region of thought, into a more secret knowledge, than the body of his brethren might share, would be exceedingly likely to regard the humbler members of the Church as creatures so far below himself in spiritual illumination, that there could not be any actual communion with them. He who believed that the mystery of sacrifice was only cognisable by the few, while yet it was a fundamental part of his faith that the sacrifice itself was for all, would gradually convince himself that only the sensual exhibition of the truth was meant for the multitude; would begin with severing that from its signification; would then impute to the bare material a sacredness which he had himself extracted from it; and so would prepare the way for results in which the student of theology and of philosophy are both

deeply interested, but in which the ordinary human being has a deeper interest than either. If the Gospel had been left to the mercy of Alexandrian doctors, it would have been in as great danger of losing its human quality, its sympathy with publicans and sinners, as it was of losing its finer and purer essence when it fell among the rough dogmatists of Carthage. Much as there was in the gentle, pure, and humble mind of Clemens to counteract this danger, it required the stronger counteraction of an opposing, and in itself perhaps a more mischievous tendency, together with the discipline of persecutions, and a direct antagonism from heathen philosophy, that it might not pass into a mere system for novices and adepts; husks being the only food provided for the first, and an intoxicating mephitic vapour being the nourishment of the other. *How the danger was checked.*

20. The phrase *eclectic* suggests a series of reflections scarcely less serious, and even alarming. The sense in which it is used by Clemens is obvious enough. He did not care for Plato, Aristotle, Pythagoras, as such; far less did he care for the opinions and conflicts of the schools which bore their names: he found in each, hints of precious truths of which he desired to avail himself; he would gather the flowers without asking in what garden they grew, the prickles he would leave for those who had a fancy for them. Eclecticism in this sense seemed only like another name for catholic wisdom. A man conscious that every thing in nature and in art was given for his learning, had a right to suck honey wherever it was to be found; he could find sweetness in it if it was hanging wild on trees and shrubs, he could admire the elaborate architecture of the cells in which it was stored. The Author of all good to man had scattered the gifts, had imparted the skill; to receive them thankfully was an act of homage to Him. But once lose the feeling of devotion and gratitude which belonged so remarkably to Clemens,—once let it be fancied that the philosopher was not a mere receiver of treasures which had been provided for him, but an ingenious chemist and compounder of various naturally unsociable ingredients, and the eclectical doctrine would lead to more self-conceit, would be more unreal and heartless, than any one of the sectarian elements out of which it was fashioned. It would want the belief and conviction which dwell, with whatever unsuitable companions, even in the narrowest theory. Many of the most vital characteristics of the original dogmas would be effaced under pretence of taking off their rough edges and fitting them into each other. In general, the superficialities and formalities of each creed would be preserved in the new system; its original and essential characteristics sacrificed. We shall have abundant illustrations *Eclecticism.* *Its perils.*

of these remarks as we proceed. Our present business is to notice some of the contemporaneous manifestations of that philosophical temper, the Christian type of which is exhibited in Clemens.

Ammonius Saccas.

21. Among the sages of Alexandria at the end of the 2d century, and the beginning of the 3d, was one person who has given occasion to much controversy. Ammonius Saccas has left no writings behind him from which we may judge what he was, or wherein lay the secret of the influence which he evidently exerted over men of great ability, and very differently educated. In fact, one main part of our knowledge respecting him is that he did not write,—at all events, that he did not put forth what he had written; and that he exacted an oath of secrecy from his hearers. No one, therefore, seems to have carried the esoteric habit of this age farther than he did. The question arises whether in doing so he started from the ground of Numenius or of Clemens,—whether his silence and reserve rested upon maxims of the Church or of the Schools. Porphyry claims him as a deserter from the Christian camp. The Christian historians of the next century do not admit the apostasy; but they do not claim Ammonius as an ally. The dispute, however it may be settled, is instructive. It shows that there was a class of men who occupied a position which might easily be misunderstood,—men who seemed to have affinities with the

His probable relation to the Christians.

teachers of the Church, who probably listened to them, and were listened to by them; who on certain points came apparently into the closest contact with them, and yet who, at some period of their life, may have diverged very markedly and widely from them,—may have even come into collision with them. It would seem exceedingly likely that Ammonius had heard the historical facts which the preachers of the Gospel believed; that he had perceived how much less the Alexandrian Christians dwelt upon them than upon the principles which those facts were said to embody,—how readily they translated the fact into a principle; that he may have conceived the possibility of dwelling exclusively upon the one without positively repudiating the other; that he may have spoken of the principles as very profound and mysterious, fit only for the most prepared and disciplined ears, and may have condemned the Christian teachers for profaning them in popular addresses; that he may have become more and more distinguished from them, and opposed to them in so far forth as they were preachers, without feeling any great repugnance to them as seekers and students; that he may have learnt at the same time from their example, that principles do need to take some concrete form, if they are to be made intelligible; that he may have considered and talked with his disciples about the different forms and media through which they might become apprehensible to the vulgar; but that at the same time he may have strongly urged the possibility of a higher and diviner intuition through which the philosopher might rise into converse with truth in its essence and nakedness; that the method which he pointed out for this end, as well as his general views respecting the other and lower method, may have been confined to the most chosen circle of his followers, who will have been forbidden, not so much from any jealousy which the master might have of his own fame, as on account of the very nature of the doctrine, to divulge. The concealment was, in fact, inevitable. A person contemplating things from this point of view must demand it if he is not inconsistent with himself.

22. While Ammonius was lecturing in Alexandria, there came to it a young man in the 27th year of his age. He had been smitten with the love of wisdom, and he wandered from doctor to doctor to find the object of his passion. He returned from each, disappointed and heavy-hearted. A friend to whom he told his grief bade him visit the school of Ammonius, whom he had not yet tried. "This," he exclaimed at the first lecture, "is the man I was seeking for." The charm was not worn out after eleven years. All our knowledge of the teacher is derived from this pupil. We should have little interest in Ammonius if it were not for the influence he exercised over Plotinus. *Plotinus.*

23. When he had taken his fill of Alexandrian doctrine, this ardent student entered the army of the Emperor Gordianus, then starting for Persia, that he might acquaint himself with the science of the Magians, and perhaps come into converse with the Brahmins. After the Emperor had been slain in Mesopotamia, Plotinus escaped with some difficulty to Antioch. In his 40th year, during the reign of the Emperor Philip, he went to Rome. All this time he had written nothing. His reverence for Ammonius and for his oath kept him from divulging the secret lore which two of his fellow disciples, Herennius and Origen, according to Porphyry, had already betrayed. He allowed, however, different students to visit him, and to ask him questions. Their various reports of his responses, as might have been expected, gave rise to no little perplexity and misrepresentation. Aurelius, who had already written out or committed to memory all the dogmas of Numenius, came to him in the fourth year of his stay at Rome, and listened to him for twenty-four years. He made a collection of scholia, or commentaries, the results of their interviews, which grew to the number of 100 volumes. But he never ventured *His education. Life by Porphyry, c. 3. His disciples.*

56 CHARACTER OF PLOTINUS.

to write down the utterances of the master himself. When Plotinus was above fifty years old, he began himself to be a writer. Porphyry joined him about nine years after; he had then composed twenty-one books. He communicated them to very few. But for Porphyry, they might never have seen the light. In the following ten years, the conversation of his two disciples brought out the books which exhibit, Porphyry thinks, the fulness of his power. He afterwards wrote nine more when it was in its decline.

24. Plotinus was therefore not chiefly a book-maker or a lecturer. His wisdom came forth in the better and more natural form of conversation. His Enneads are resolutions of difficulties which had occurred to himself or to others. There is no reason to doubt that he was,—what Apollo, in a somewhat lengthy oracle faithfully reported by his disciple, and what that disciple, on the equally satisfactory evidence of his own experience, testifies him to have been—" good and gentle and benignant in a very high degree, and pleasant in all his intercourse." He seems to have won the affection of many who could have understood nothing of his teaching,—to have given them sensible advice about mundane affairs, and even to have been a careful steward of the monies which they entrusted to him. But of his own body he was utterly negligent. No entreaties could persuade him to allow a portrait of himself to be taken. " Was not humiliating enough to be obliged to carry a shadow about with him, without having a shadow made of that shadow ?" He declined all the natural remedies when he was afflicted with a serious sickness, refused animal food, abstained from baths. He was attacked with a pestilence which prevailed in Italy, lost the use of his hands, his feet, and his voice; his sufferings being terribly aggravated, it would appear, from his rejection of all alleviations. He at last left the city, was taken to the estate of a friend in Campania, and died, as Eustochius reported, exclaiming, " I am striving to bring the divine thing which is in us, to the divine which is in the universe."

25. Whether Plotinus uttered these words or not, as his spirit was departing, they certainly express the effort of his life, and the object of his philosophy. We have spoken of him as in one respect resembling Socrates,—that he conversed rather than wrote. He himself supposed that he resembled Socrates in most things,—that he was, in fact, restoring to the world the very spirit which had spoken in him when his friends were gathered about his couch, and he was thanking the Athenian dicasts for the emancipation which they were preparing for him. Yet no two men were ever really more strongly contrasted with each other, not merely in their characters, but in

their whole method. If Socrates sought for the Being, for the eternal substance which no images could present to him, and which he could only truly embrace while he turned away from shadows and phantoms, he hoped to attain this blessing for himself, or to show his disciples how they might attain it, by testing the words which they spoke, by entering into converse with the tools of every ordinary craft, by acknowledging the worth of the most vulgar and earthly things. Unless he could arrive at the truth of each thing which presented itself to him, he had no hope of arriving at the absolute truth. All his genial habits of mind, his sympathy, his humour, became thus the inseparable ministers of his philosophy, nay almost constituted it. They kept him in communion with facts; they would not allow him to mistake that which is, for the creation of his own mind; they made him seek for a road by which every man might rise to the height which he was climbing. *The Socratic method.*

26. Plotinus was born into an age when it was impossible, or at least unspeakably difficult, to begin where Socrates began. The Christian teachers had been asserting pertinaciously, for two centuries, that there had been an actual revelation of the most transcendent mysteries; that princes and beggars might have communion with the Divine Nature; might be partakers of it. Every sage was bound to say whether this was his end, and how he hoped to attain it. He was forced to commence with a theology, and to explain how he connected it with the condition of humanity. Supposing he utterly discarded the doctrine of God taking human flesh, he must find some substitute for that doctrine; his ethics, his physics, his dialectics, would all depend upon it. If we forget those thoughts respecting the Absolute Being, and the Being in contact with man or with matter, which Numenius and Clemens have brought before us, the processes in the mind of Plotinus will be quite unintelligible to us. We shall suppose that he is wilfully and industriously combining some old notions of divinity with his Platonism, whereas the conjunction was inevitable. He could escape neither the vagueness and impersonality which will often seem characteristic of his highest speculations, nor those allusions to secondary powers and divinities, to a race of inferior dæmons which may seem to us to contain the germs of a very gross superstition. How the mixture afterwards worked, what kind of influence it produced through two centuries, we shall have to consider hereafter. The real key to all the subsequent developments of the school lies in the writings of its illustrious founder. *Why Plotinus could not adopt it.*

27. Plotinus committed the arrangement of his books to Porphyry. He disposed them according to subjects, sacrificing the chronology of the writings—which we might have been glad *The Enneads.*

58   DISPOSITION OF THIS PHILOSOPHY.

<small>Life, c. 24.</small>

<small>The Ethical.</small>

<small>The Physical.</small>

<small>Ontology.</small>

<small>Virtue, whether divine.</small>

to trace—to philosophical symmetry. " I disposed them," he says, " into six Enneads, gladly availing myself of the two perfect numbers (6 and 9)." He hoped that the reader would rise to the more difficult problems by a regular gradation. His first Enneas contains what he calls the more purely ethical discussions. It embraces such topics as these—What is the Animal and what is the Man ?—On Virtues—On Dialectics— On Happiness—Whether Blessedness consists in the lengthening out of Time—On the Beautiful—On the Primary Good and the other goods—Whence spring Evils—On a reasonable Departure out of Life.

The next Enneas is on physical questions—Of the World— Of Circular Motion—Whether the Stars have any activity—On the Potential and the Actual—On Quality and Form or Species —An answer to those who think the Maker of the World, or the World itself, to be Evil.

As this division includes several topics which Aristotle would certainly have assigned to metaphysics rather than physics, so it is not very obvious where Porphyry draws the line between it and the succeeding one, which he says still treats of the Κόσμος, but includes those subjects which have relation to it, not merely those which are embraced in it. This Enneas discusses Fate—Providence—Of the Dæmon to whose lot we have fallen (τὸν εἰληχότος ἡμᾶς δαίμονος)—Of Love—Of Eternity and Time—Of Nature, Contemplation, and the One. The editor excuses himself for introducing some of these titles here; his defence is scarcely satisfactory. The fourth Enneas treats entirely of the Soul—On the Substance of the Soul—On Sensation and Memory—On the Immortality of the Soul—On the Descent of the Soul into Bodies. The fifth ascends into the transcendent region: it treats of Reason, and Being, and Ideas. The last speaks of the kinds of Being—Of the Identity of Being, and Unity—Of Numbers—How there comes to be Plurality of Ideas—Of the Good.

Porphyry regards the first three Enneads as forming one section of the work, the fourth and fifth another, the sixth complete in itself.

28. Union with the Divinity being the one object of Plotinus, various questions suggest themselves to him, in which ethics and theology are intimately combined. The second book of the first Ennead, " On Virtues," brings these especially before us. It is doubtless by virtues that we are to be assimilated to the divine nature. But can virtues be predicated of that nature ? Can there be courage in a Being who has nothing to fear ? self-restraint in one who has nothing to desire ? Perhaps a distinction might be drawn between the noetic and the political

virtues, between those which have reference to the pure objects of the intellect, and those which have reference to the conditions of human society. Perhaps too there might be some god to whom such qualities might be ascribed; say the Soul of the world, or the presiding principle in it. Still such explanations hardly satisfy the enquirer. Is it possible, then, that there may be obtained through virtue some likeness to One who himself does not possess it, or possesses it under quite different conditions; as it is not absolutely necessary to suppose that a substance from which heat is received has itself the sensation of heat. If one examines that illustration more deeply, Plotinus thinks it may suggest another inference, that the heat is innate in that which communicates the heat; in that which receives it, derivative; and that similarly there ought to be, if not virtue, yet something higher than virtue, in him from whom man proceeds. The actual visible house, he says, is not the same with that which is in the mind; yet one has the likeness of the other, and derives from it its order and harmony. These qualities of the building cannot be said to exist in their noetic or spiritual counterpart. So, though there may be no need of what we call virtue in God, the possession of it may be that which brings us into consent with his nature. The result at which the discussion arrives is this: that virtues are purgative, that the worth of them is to separate that in man which is capable of converse with the noetic, the essentially pure, from that which is animal and earthly; that by this process they prepare the reason to come into contact with its highest object. Virtue being in the Soul which is in connection with the body, and liable to its influence, not in the pure Reason, or in that which lies beyond it, is a perpetual exercise of restraint and cleansing for the purpose of disengaging the man from his lower companion, and fitting him for—the question cannot be avoided—for what? Plotinus answers, for becoming a god. Supposing him to reach such a point as that he shall be wholly free from voluntary transgression, but shall still be exposed to assaults from anger, desire, and the like, he may be only a Dæmon, possessing still a twofold nature, in which the higher is supreme. But if he could overcome his propensities entirely, then he would be simply a god, " one of those that follow the Highest God." *The difficulty stated and resolved.* *Virtue a means of attaining godhead.*

29. The book on Dialectics, which follows this on Virtues, should be read in connection with the Platonic Phædrus, that the student may appreciate the difference between the ancient teacher and the reviver, and may acquit Plotinus of any servile imitation. He is not open to that charge; what he inherited he certainly reduced into possession, and yet no one more *Dialectics of Plotinus.*

reverently and frankly confesses his obligations. The question is, by what process we are to ascend into that region of the good, to that original principle, which has been shown before to be the right goal of our pilgrimage. The man may be looked upon in three stages of progress, or rather he may be said to have originally descended into three types of being, out of which he is gradually to rise. "First, the Musician, easily impressed and carried on towards the beautiful, but without the power of being directly moved by it; readily affected towards sounds, as cowards are by noises, and catching at the beautiful, which lies close at hand in them; ever flying from the discordant, and seeking for the harmonious and the proportionate; may be lifted above the sensible sounds, and measures, and forms, to the beauty that is above them; may be taught the noetic harmony which lies beneath the things towards which he is carried away; may attain, not to some beautiful thing, but to *the* Beauty." Plotinus intimates that there may be yet a further passage for him out of this region into the truths of pure science, of which he is ignorant, though in a manner he possesses them. "Next the Lover, into whom the musician may very probably be converted. He has a certain recollection of beauty; but being outside of it, he is not able to learn what it is. But being stricken by the beautiful things which come under his sight, he is carried about them. You must teach him not to fly round and round about one body, with the danger of always descending lower towards it; you must bring him by reason to compare bodies together, pointing out to him that which is the same in all; and you must tell him that it is different from the bodies, and that it comes from elsewhere, and that it dwells in others more than in these; shewing him how beautiful Studies may be, and how beautiful Laws may be. Thus the Lover may become habituated to that which is without body, discovering it in arts and sciences, and virtues. Then you must make him feel that there is one Beauty in all things, and you must teach him how they arise out of it. Then, from the virtues, teach him how to ascend to the pure Reason, and after into Being itself, and there he may move along on his upward journey. Last of all, the Philosopher: ready by nature, and as it were already furnished with wings; not needing to sever them from matter like the others; disposed already to ascend to that which is above; but still being perplexed, he wants some one to point the way. To him you must give mathematics, for the discipline of his intellect and of his incorporeal faith. These he will readily receive, being greedy of knowledge, and seeing that he has a natural aptitude for virtue. And after mathematics you must give him dialectics; you must make him thoroughly a dialectician. But what is this dialectic which must be given in some proportion to the musician and the lover also? "It is," answers Plotinus, "the habit which enables one to say about each thing what its peculiarity is, wherein it differs from other things, what there is in common between them, and where each of these things is, and whether that is which is, and how many are the things that are, and again the things that are not, and how they differ from those that are. It discourses," he says, "also concerning the Good and concerning the Not-good, and how many things fall under the Good, and what is manifestly Eternal, and what is not so. It aims in all things at science, not at opinion, restraining the soul from its wanderings after sensible things, disciplining it to the noetic; there lies its whole occupation. And whence," he asks, "has this science its principles? The answer is, that the pure reason gives them, and the soul, by different processes of discipline, is made capable of receiving them. The dialectical habit is the highest and most honourable of all that man can possess, and it is exercised about the highest and noblest things. It results from the combination of the prudential faculty with the pure reason, the one referring to Being, the other carrying you beyond Being. Is it, then, the same thing with philosophy? No; but it is the most essential and glorious part of philosophy. It must not be imagined to be a mere instrument of philosophy. It does not invent propositions about things, but it deals with the substances themselves. Pure Being, if we can bear the contradiction, is the *material* with which it works."

Dialectic what?

30. If we suppose that there is a point at which the master of Plotinus was in contact with the Christian teachers of Alexandria, the passages which we have selected from the Enneads may perhaps assist us in understanding and feeling the reason of their divergence. The necessity of emancipation would be recognised alike by both. One as much as the other might describe it as the emancipation of a spirit from the chains of sense: one as much as the other might think that the man was gradually to ascend into the region which was intended for him out of a material world in which he was sunk, and the phantoms of which were continually misleading and detaining him. But the moment the Church teacher spoke to the man, not of an oppression that was arising from a lower nature attached to him, but of an evil that dwelt in himself, his language would become partly disagreeable, partly unintelligible to the new school. A dialectician, even a lover or a musician, who has a perception of some beautiful and transcendent object, will meet with a certain sympathy from Plotinus. He will help him to rise into a more ethereal, one would fancy

Relation of Plotinus to Christians.

also, into rather a colder region, than that from which he has escaped,—one in which his attachment to every thing distinct and particular would be lost in the vision of the absolute and universal. But if the highest of these forms of being, or either of the subordinate ones, besides being philosophical, or loving, or musical, should chance to be human, and to be conscious of certain inward torments and distempers, which, though very closely mingling with all his passions and pursuits, have nevertheless a character and root of their own; if any one of them should ever be brought to feel " it is myself that is my torment; it is from that, I want to be delivered," one cannot help fearing that the prescriptions of Plotinus would be found not quite adequate to the seriousness of the emergency. The inevitable result of them, one must think, is to re-establish that barrier between the man and the philosopher which it seemed to us that all the better and more earnest teachers of the old world had wished to remove, and to which they only submitted through a hard necessity; a distinction which, however plausible and hopeful, does, in fact, quite as much injury to the select band whom it glorifies, as to the mass whom it scorns, making the highest point to which they reach, one where there is pure light without the slightest warmth. It is most satisfactory to think that neither Plotinus himself, nor perhaps any of his followers, ever succeeded in reaching this point. They continued to be men, not such Dæmons or Gods as they dreamed they might become.

Sense of evil, of self.

Philosophers still men.

True education of the Dialectician.

31. In saying this, we do not in the least design to disparage the dialectic of which Plotinus speaks so ably, and of which Plato had spoken with immeasurably more freedom, precision, and practical sense, before him. To cultivate that habit of which he speaks, that wonderful habit of distinguishing the substance within from that which encircles it,—the reality from the counterfeit,—must be indeed the highest effort of a sound and practical education. The complete possession of it must be the greatest gift which can be conferred upon a man. None of the means for obtaining it which Plotinus has suggested, ought to be slighted by those who can avail themselves of them. What we venture to doubt is, whether those means will be found sufficient, whether we shall ever have a consummate dialectician, in this sense of the word, who has not been engaged in a much more close death embrace with evil than a Neo-Platonist would have thought desirable or graceful; whether he must not have much more understood the evils of other men as his own, than could be right for those who were striving to be gods; whether a simple clownish man, who had entered heartily into this strife, would not have a dialectical discernment which a person well trained in mathematics, and

that excellent discipline which Plotinus recommends, might after all utterly want. Meantime, though these observations are needful to connect the different sides of our history together, let no one make them an excuse for not profiting by the lessons which an eminent man, who has worked zealously in one direction, can give us. It would certainly be a poor evidence of any one having acquired greater humility in another school, that he had been brought to despise Plotinus.

32. It must not be inferred from what we have said of his internal sense of evil, that we think he has treated the subject of evil less successfully than other moralists, or that we regard this as the weak part of his discourses. There is no book we should more recommend to the attention of our readers than the eighth of the first Ennead, in which he grapples with the question, What is evil, and whence comes it? Plotinus states fairly and honestly the different suggestions which present themselves to all serious and reflecting minds when they approach this abyss. Is it positive? Is it only a failure and eclipse of good? Is it in matter? Is it in the soul? Must there not be an original archetypal evil, from which the different forms of it have proceeded, and wherein they terminate? What is the real conflict of life? What is the victory? What is the ultimate defeat? No one, we think, can follow him through the discussion of these questions without thankfulness for the light which he has thrown on them, and a feeling that some further solution may be and must be had. We should be doing little justice to Plotinus if we stated the formal results to which this inquiry led him. The interest of the book, and that which is the most agreeable characteristic of the writer, is, that he does not put forth a set of dogmatic resolutions, but talks over the different points with himself, giving us glimpses into the processes of his mind, and enabling us to see that it has earnestly fought with a number of intellectual giants, though he may not have been in that thickest and hottest part of the fight where the question is, whether the man must not part with himself in order that he may part with evil. *His theory of evil.*

33. Oftentimes the reader may be inclined to suppose that Plotinus must have had some sympathy with the Christian Gnostics. He feels so strongly that the fall of the Soul consists in its becoming subject to matter, that it is lost when it is completely immersed in matter, that it only rises into communion with the perfect good when it becomes separated from matter; that we might suppose him to agree with them, that the source of evil lies in matter. This would itself be a false inference. He believes that the tendency of the soul to sink into that which is below itself, is not derived from that into which it *His dislike to the Gnostics.*

sinks; that tendency has its root somewhere else; where, he does not distinctly affirm. But even supposing he had agreed with the Gnostics so far, he would not have been at all nearer to their assertion that the World or Order is evil. He does not look upon this Order as material; nothing seemed to him so utterly shocking, as the notion that it could be anything less than perfect, divine, eternal. The ninth book of the second Ennead is devoted to the confutation of the Gnostical dogma upon this point. "The men," he says, "who complain of the nature of the world, know not what they are doing, and whither their boldness is carrying them. This is because they know not the arrangement of the different portions of this order, its first and second and third degrees, down to the lowest of all, and that it does not become us to find fault with those things that are worse than the first, but meekly to conform ourselves to the universal nature, pressing on still towards the best, and casting aside those empty terrors, such as some are possessed with when they contemplate the great circles of the world, which in truth are procuring all blessings to them. What have these really terrible, as they terrify those who are ignorant of true reason, and who have not submitted themselves to the discipline of science? For what if these forms which they behold are of a fiery nature? We do not therefore need to fear them, seeing that they are in harmony with the nature of the universe, and with the earth. But it behoves them rather to look to those souls, in virtue of which they deem themselves estimable, though they ought to know that their bodies too, excelling as they do in greatness and beauty, are servants and fellow-workers in the scheme of nature, rightly following those things which have rightly the pre-eminence, filling up the universe, and being great elements of it. And if men have an honour beyond all other animals, much more should these things have their honour which exist in the great whole, not as rulers of it, but as supplying to it grace and order. And we are not to demand that all in the world should be good, and to fall into grumbling because this is not possible at once, nor to call the imperfect and lesser good an evil. If one calls nature evil because it is not sensation, and sensation because it is not the reasoning power of the soul, one must call that evil too, seeing that the soul is lower than the pure mind, and there is something higher than that."

This is a summary of the general argument. All things are good in the Order. They become evil when they fall out of it, losing their relations, proportions, sequences. To speak of an evil world, or an evil order, is therefore a contradiction.

The world divine.

34. A faithful disciple of Plotinus would say that we had only touched the outskirts of his doctrine, and not ascended into its more mystical heights, unless we spoke more distinctly of those passages which refer to the pure and essential One, the *The One* object towards which the emancipated philosopher is continually moving. But we have given our readers hints which will enable them to perceive how necessarily this was the end which every thinker of the third century set before himself,—Plotinus, more than others, only so far as he more distinctly apprehended that which others mixed with various intermediate and subordinate purposes. The last extract will prove that he recognised these subordinate purposes as being good for themselves, and the other as only attainable by the illuminated few. It was but twice or thrice in his life that Plotinus claimed to have had a direct vision of the perfect and absolute One. In general, it was only some dæmon or lower god whom even he was enabled *Dæmons.* to contemplate. The existence of such dæmons, and their position in the great economy of the universe, was a subject which forced itself continually on the Neo-Platonist and his disciples. The gods whom the old Athenian had accepted from his country's traditions, but which he tried to divest of the corrupt qualities which had been imputed to them by the minds of their worshippers, must be reproduced in this later age of the world as the necessary completions of a philosophical theory,—as the only steps of a ladder between earth and heaven. Each of the old gods had a place in the new philosophical Pantheon; but it was a most insecure place, which he owed confessedly to the inability of men to divest themselves of accidents, and localities, and affections; to their want of that highest perception which would have made them content with a mere spiritual essence. The Platonist, however, was soon obliged to give them a more tangible existence, otherwise he would have had no standing ground against the Church, which he more and more felt to be the most serious obstacle to the general recognition, even to the secure and comfortable maintenance, of his doctrine.

35. There are one or two facts concerning Plotinus recorded *The new* by his biographer which we have reserved for a separate consi- *Republic.* deration, as they greatly illustrate the history of his time and of his school. The first is this. Plotinus was greatly honoured by the Emperor Gallienus and his wife Salolina. Availing himself of this friendship he besought him to rebuild a city in Campania, said to have been formerly a resort of philosophers, but now in decay; to associate with it the surrounding country; to permit the future citizens to be governed by the laws of Plato, and the city itself to be called Platonopolis. There he had promised that he would retire with his companions; and

F

the wish of the philosopher would have been speedily accomplished, if some of those who were familiar with the Emperor, through envy, or dislike, or some other bad motive, had not prevented it.

Attempted imitation of Plato.
36. How much does Neo-Platonism owe to these ill-natured courtiers of Gallienus! A more fatal experiment than the Campanian one could scarcely have been made; one which would have more exposed all the practical weakness of the system. No doubt, Plotinus fancied that he had his master's example to guide him in this case as in all others. Did not Plato hope to realise his Republic by the help of Dionysius? If he ever had so wild a dream, the dispersion of it is recorded in the same tradition which imputes it to him. Plotinus need not have taken the first part of the story and forgotten the sequel. But the fact that a copy of that weakest and most disastrous portion of Plato's life was attempted, is an evidence, we conceive, first, that Plotinus perceived that a Republic was a necessary complement of the Platonic philosophy; next, that he entirely mistook what the relation was between his dialectics and his politics. Plato, as we tried to prove in the sketch of ancient philosophy, was a scientific enquirer into the nature and conditions under which all society must exist,—not the inventor of a particular society.

Why unsuccessful.
All that Plotinus meant, so far as we can gather from his faithful and intelligent disciple,—all that he certainly would have accomplished, if his success had equalled his highest aspirations,—would have been to construct a city with a fine name which should have been a fit refuge for philosophers who wanted a world of their own unlike that in which ordinary mortals were dwelling. Platonopolis was to have been a place for the élite of the universe—a place in which they would have tried to rule and legislate—where doctors would have been kings, and school formulas would have invented sanctions for themselves —where old rivalries and old crimes would speedily have shown that sages are men, and that they would be much more sage if they admitted the fact boldly, and considered what is involved in it.

Implicit faith of Plotinus.
37. If Plotinus hoped in this way to establish something which would be far better and more sublime than those churches into which he and Ammonius had seen so many vulgar men admitted, he found also a substitute for the records or sacred books to which those churches appealed. Our readers must be aware by this time that the difference between the Neo-Platonists and the Christians did not consist in any independence of judgment which was claimed by the former. No Father could quote St. Paul or St. John with more absolute or child-like deference than that with which Plotinus habitually quotes Plato. His

name is not often mentioned, but you find sentence after sentence beginning " He says ;" and you never doubt for a moment that an oracle is appealed to, which may require elucidation but from which there is no dissent. We shall find, the further we proceed with our history, continual instances of the same kind of subjection on the part, not of weak men, who cannot and dare not think for themselves, but of the most coherent and courageous thinkers. The discovery ought to make us pause before we adopt some very current and popular notions as to the nature and limits of freedom in speculation. If we suppose freedom to be impossible, or not desirable for men, we should commit one huge blunder. If we suppose that a guide or a text-book is necessarily unfavourable to it, we may commit as great a one. *Intellectual freedom.*

38. One Olympius, an Alexandrian, Porphyry tells us, who was for a short time a disciple of Ammonius, despised Plotinus, aspiring to the first dignity in philosophy. Nay, so far did he go in his enmity, that he strove to crush him with magical arts. But he soon found that the experiment turned against himself; and he told his associates that the soul of Plotinus had such mighty power that it caused all assaults upon him to react upon those who were hurting him. In fact, all the limbs of Olympius became contracted. Miracles, therefore, we see were closely allied with the new philosophy. Whether there was to be a whole system of Magic and Astrology connected with it, was a question to be considered afterwards. But the power of the man who was approaching the condition of a god to act upon the souls or bodies of other creatures, was not a matter of doubt with those who held the least exaggerated opinions on this subject. The power rested in that communion with higher natures which the philosopher had attained; nor does he seem to have felt that there was any thing strange or awful in such a power, or that it might not be used for mere personal ends. On another occasion, an Egyptian priest, who had come to Rome and desired to display his wisdom, persuaded Plotinus to call into his presence the dæmon who was holding familiar converse with him. The Temple of Isis having been chosen for the invocation, at the summons of Plotinus, to the admiration of the Egyptian, a god instead of an inferior dæmon appeared. This fact, like the other, is related without timidity, or any attempt to confirm it by evidence. It is worthy of being remembered, not merely as illustrating the theology of the school, but as showing how soon that theology which aspired to be so ethereal and spiritual might become mixed with all the sensible apparitions of ordinary superstition. *Magic has resisted.* *Divine apparitions.*

39. Porphyry was not naturally inclined to dæmonology. A

story which he tells of a discourse which he made in answer to a philosopher who had maintained the most grovelling notions respecting love and self-indulgence—a discourse which won for him the highest reward he could receive, the approving smile of Plotinus—shows that he had strong and healthy moral instincts. His dislike of the common herd, probably the secret of that dislike to Christianity which became so much more definite and vehement in him than it had been in his master, was gratified by all his philosophical studies; he must have been, therefore, very unwilling that they should minister to vulgar tastes and to the passion for the marvellous. Yet to separate the communion with divine natures, wherein consisted the prize and consummation of the new philosophy, from the practices of the magician, which had been hard at all times, was never harder than in the third century after Christ. Was the ascent of the man into the divine region to produce no effect upon himself or upon the world? Was the spiritual in no way to assert its right to control and govern the material as well as to be emancipated from its dominion? The suffering man, of whom the ignorant Christians spoke, was alleged to have healed the sick and cast out devils: must not the divine sage be able to show that he can work greater, of course less common and useful, miracles than these? Porphyry wavered between the necessity of asserting such a power for him that he might prove his elevation or confound adversaries, and the imminent danger of introducing all those dark imaginations and practices against which ancient philosophers had protested,—which their modern disciple Apollonius, at least in the commencement of his career, had set himself to encounter.

The Empirical or Sceptical school.

40. Like other seekers of middle ways, Porphyry soon found himself hardly pressed on the right hand and on the left. No century has been without its school of experimental as well as of mystical philosophy. The third had physicians, who studied, as well as they could, the facts of nature,—who were led by the observation of them to protest against the traders in mysteries —who gradually were led on to disbelieve all mysteries. The time is not come for speaking of them; the influence of their physical speculations on the history of moral philosophy can only be understood in a later age. The Platonic doctrine is *the* characteristic one of the period with which we are occupied. Still, it is necessary to allude to the empirical school, that we may understand why Porphyry, who must have been unable to understand many of its arguments, would have despised its facts, would have been shocked at its incredulity, might be tempted to crave help even from it (if he had known how to use the help) against a more popular and dangerous class of foes which he

discovered in his own camp. Merely to argue against the Christians, merely to show how portions of the old mythology might be made to give out a philosophical meaning, could never satisfy the Greek and Roman, still less the Egyptian and Oriental sages of the empire. Philosophy must resuscitate Paganism, or it would not fulfil its mission. If it did not explain and justify the operations of the old priest, if it could not establish an offensive and defensive alliance with him—it could not maintain its own ground, it would have to be cast aside as a mere dry ungenerative speculation. Such was the language which began to be heard more and more distinctly in the schools which adopted the theories of Ammonius or Plotinus; such was the tendency which Porphyry, after dallying with it for a time, at last girded himself to encounter. *Platonism becoming mythological.*

41. The form in which he expressed his objections was cautious, but perhaps the more offensive on that account. His letter to Anebon, an Egyptian prophet, or priest, is a clever, sagacious, well-digested statement of the difficulties which a philosopher discovered, as well in the popular conceptions respecting the gods and dæmons, as in the whole mysteries of Theurgy. This letter, and the answer to it, form so memorable an event in philosophical history, that we think they are entitled to more attention than many larger works written by much greater men than Porphyry or his correspondent. *Letter to Anebon.*

42. Porphyry starts from the assumption that there are gods. But he wants to know their distinctions and peculiarities. Does the distinction arise from their actions or their passions; or from their relation to different bodies,—according to a maxim which seems to have been then recognised, that the gods had ethereal bodies, dæmons aerial, souls terrestrial? The next question refers to the attribution of place to the gods: how is this compatible with their infinity? Next their liability to passions, upon which the whole doctrine of Theurgy would seem to depend; since how can those be conciliated or appeased who are not susceptible of impressions from without? And since invocations are addressed to the higher as well as the lower gods, since sacrifices are especially directed to them, they must be treated as subject to passions like the rest,—not as pure minds or intellects. Are gods and dæmons distinguished by the possession or absence of body? How is it that some of the gods are beneficent, and some malevolent? In what way does a hero differ from a dæmon or from a soul? How do you distinguish the appearance of a god, of an angel, of a dæmon, of a soul? For the very highest gods are presented to us in images and sensible forms. *The distinction of gods.*

43. These questions Porphyry considers profoundly important,

seeing that all good lies in the knowledge of the gods,—all darkness in the ignorance of them. There are a set of subordinate questions arising out of these. The first refers to prophecy. Putting aside the knowledge of the future which comes through dreams, wherein the mind and body are passive, how can all those ecstasies which are produced by noises or mephitic vapours, or how can the knowledge which is obtained from the flights of birds, or the entrails of beasts, be esteemed divine? Is a god, or an angel, or a dæmon, the author of prophecy and apparitions; or may they originate from the soul itself: or may they be attributed to a substance compounded of the soul and of some divine inspiration? May there not be certain affinities and relations between bodies, and may not these bodies produce some mutual pre-cognitions? And may not Nature itself, or Art, working with these, produce the results which are attributed to dæmons or gods? Is there any truth in the notion that there may be a species of deceiving natures assuming various forms which counterfeit the gods and dæmons and the souls of the departed,—which can work no good, but hinder those who are aiming at virtue,— which are full of pride, and rejoice in incense and sacrifices? The next question touches the very heart of Egyptian worship and divination. We call for the help of those whom we esteem more august and divine than ourselves; yet they obey the call of those who are lower and worse than themselves. The contradiction is expanded through a number of particulars; well-known practices, or statements of priests of high authority, being alleged to prove that not only some common dæmon or departed spirit, but that sun, moon, and stars, were treated as obnoxious to the threats as well as the petitions of the priests. No doubt, suggests the questioner, all these things may have a symbolical force,—they may indicate the various powers and changes of these bodies; but then the explanation should be produced, and it should be shown what the influences and changes of the sun and moon had to do with the incantations; and particularly why those incantations should be couched in peculiar, commonly barbarous phrases. For supposing the Deity attends to the signification of that which is said, the thought expressed in the words would be sufficient for him in whatever terms it were conveyed. Next, Anebon is asked whether the Egyptians consider the First Cause Nous, or something above it; whether it is alone or united with any other or others; whether it is corporeal or incorporeal; whether it is the same with the Demiurgus or before him; whether all things came from one or from more; whether they acknowledge matter or not; whether it is generated or eternal; what are the primary bodies. Next, he desires to hear about the dæmon who belongs to each man; whether he is an efflux, or a life, or a power; whether he may be known, or whether it is impossible to discover him. Are there different dæmons,—one presiding over our health, another over our beauty, and so forth? If so, is there one common superintendent of them? May there be one of the mind, another of the body? May there be one beneficent and one malevolent? Is it not possible that the dæmon may be part of the mind itself, and that the εὐδαίμων is the man who has a wise mind? Waxing bolder, he asks, in conclusion, whether there may not be another way to blessedness besides theurgy; nay, may not the whole business of theurgy be somewhat deceptive, seeing that people may have the possession of divine prophecy without being blessed, and may know of things to come without knowing how to make use of them? And certainly, if the god or the dæmon does not help us to blessedness, but only to the knowledge of the future, he is not a good dæmon or god, and the whole looks like an invention of mortals. The dæmon within us.

44. The person who answers these questions of Porphyry's calls himself Abammon, the teacher of Anebon. Who he was must be left among the mysteries of which he treats. It has been assumed that he was Iamblichus, because Iamblichus became ultimately the head and representative of that division of the Neo-Platonists which made Theurgy an essential part of philosophy. For practical purposes, Abammon is of more importance to us than his successor, for he has gathered together and reduced into method all that can be said in favour of the principle which Porphyry had sought to undermine, and which was destined to triumph over his objections. Abammon or Iamblichus.

45. The authorities from which the advocate for the priest proceeds, are the traditional theological dogmas of the Assyrians and Egyptians, with the speculations of Hermes, these being the sources from which Pythagoras and Plato are assumed to have drawn their wisdom. The author proposes to discuss each subject according to its proper nature; theological questions theologically, theurgical theurgically, philosophical philosophically. An exception is taken at the outset to Porphyry's language, which involves the most important consequences. You admit that there are gods. You have no business to speak so. It is not a question for a man's judgment whether there are or not. There is an innate knowledge concerning the gods which is beyond all judgment and every exercise of our will,—which precedes reason and demonstration. It is united from the beginning to its own proper cause, and is implied in that effort of the soul after the good which is part of its substance. There is a divine contact of the man with the Divinity, which, in fact, The book περὶ μυστηρίων c. 1 & 2.

72   THE INWARD CONTACT WITH THE GODS.

supersedes knowledge; the knowledge is lost or extinguished in the thing known. This principle does not only apply to the first or fundamental Being; it applies also to the dæmons and heroes. The notion of opposition, of that which is supplied in our logical forms of affirmation and denial, has nothing to do with their nature, or with the relations in which they stand to man. An objection growing out of this is taken to the second question about the properties of the different gods. Porphyry is applying notions of property and accident where they cannot apply; viz. to things uncompounded. To them sequence does not belong. All things that have to do with the higher natures must be contemplated in reference to their *being*. They must be judged by themselves; not by the condition of other natures which are below them. The question of Porphyry must be answered by an examination, not of individuals, but of kinds. We can distinguish various kinds of gods, of dæmons, of heroes, of souls; we can affirm wherein the differences between them consist. To this task Abammon proceeds. There is an absolute super-essential Good, and there is a Good which is according to the essence or the nature of the thing which possesses it. The former is the special characteristic of the gods. It belongs to each order of the gods, it preserves their proper ranks and distributions, it is not to be severed from their nature, it is the same in all. Souls, even those that rule bodies, and which before their birth were constituted eternal, possess neither the essential Good nor the super-essential; but there comes upon them a sort of efflux and habit proceeding from it. These being the two extremes, the order of heroes lies between; closely connected with human souls, but far excelling them in power and virtue. Still above these, in nearest relation to the gods yet much beneath them, are the dæmons, who bring forth into action their invisible good, and accomplish the works which are in conformity with it. That which is unspeakable becomes in them pronounced; what is without form they show forth in forms. We attribute to the gods unity; divisibility to souls. Heroes and dæmons then have a relation both to gods and to souls; they have fellowship with both, but they are liable to incline and turn aside to those inferior things which they produce and govern.

46. The whole question of Porphyry respecting the ethereal, aerial, and terrestrial gods, is thrown aside with indignation and contempt; all such corporeal divisions and limitations being utterly inconsistent with the divine nature So far from looking upon these as necessary to theurgy, they are declared to be incompatible with it. How could we invoke beings who live in regions altogether remote from us,—with whom men have nothing

Marginalia:
Theology above Logic. c. 3 & 4.
c. 5, 6, 7.
Dæmons, Heroes, Souls.
Material division. c. 8.

THE GODS NOT SUBJECT TO PASSIONS.

to do, by whom the world has been deserted? In truth all things are full of the gods. The Divinity illuminates heaven and earth, holy cities and places, divine shrines, just as the sun illuminates all the corners of the universe which he looks upon. The author of the book on Mysteries rises into real eloquence while he denounces the notion of comprehending and dividing the divine essence as absolutely monstrous, profane, and irrational.

47. Abammon equally rejects Porphyry's notion that the gods must be subject to passions if they receive sacrifices and are moved by prayers. He denies that even souls considered in their pure essence have anything to do with passions. Nevertheless he does not shrink from defending even the grosser and more impure symbols of Egyptian worship. The general ground of apology for offerings is, that they are medicinal to the human spirit, and help to emancipate it from the evils to which its connection with the body subjects it. The particular excuse for the symbols which presume evil and corruption, is, that they serve the same purpose as the sight of other men's offences or sorrows in the drama,—they help to deliver us from our own, affording besides an outlet for passions which would be more dangerous and virulent if they were wholly repressed. The defence of prayers and invocations rests on a far deeper principle, and has less the character of special pleading. It is not because the gods are subject to passions, that invocations unite the priest to them; but through the mysterious friendship or affinity which holds the universe together, they produce a community of indissoluble harmony. They do not incline the mind of the gods to men, but they make men fit for converse with the gods. Still more remarkable is the explanation of the divine anger and of propitiation. "We ourselves," he says, "turn away the care of the gods from us, hiding ourselves in the noon-day, bringing darkness upon ourselves, depriving ourselves of the good gift of the gods. Propitiation restores us to the divine communion; instead of presuming passion in the *gods*, it delivers *us* from it." The alleged necessities of the gods are explained in an equally courageous and noble manner. There is a necessity in a perfect and gracious Being of love and companionship; that necessity does not belong only to beings subject to change and passion, but most to those who are freest from them. Every thing being grounded upon this fellowship and sympathy of men with the gods, it is a mistake to say that animal offerings imply an animal nature in *them*. The use of particular sensible objects may betoken and satisfy that connection, and may contain a divine, not an earthly significance.

Passions in gods.
c. 10, 11, 12.

c. 12.

c. 13.

c. 14.

EVIL PARTICULAR NOT UNIVERSAL.

c. 17.
Goodness inherent in godhead.
c. 18.

48. To Porphyry's question, how the sun and moon should be gods, if gods are incorporeal, the answer is, that the gods being pure intelligences, can assume bodies without injury to their intellectual natures, and that there are celestial bodies which are specially cognate to the incorporeal substance of the gods, bodies which express their energies and imitate the regularity and uniformity of their substance. To his still more serious demand, whether some gods are benevolent and some malevolent, the reply is decided—the gods are perfectly good. The virtues of the inferior gods derived out of the primary essence are however different, and may often seem to be of opposite kinds. The virtue of Chronos, for instance, is contractive; that of Ares motive. When these powers are brought to bear upon bodies, cold may be the effect of one, heat of the other: but evil only begins when these different powers come into connection with divided and material natures. A weak body may be grievously affected by the heat of the sun, yet the heat of the sun is good; all evil, therefore, belongs to particulars, not to the universal. The author proceeds to explain the relation between the purely intellectual gods, and those to which bodies are attached, making the former the ground and origin of the latter, affirming their perfect unity, and tracing the process by which the lower, perceiving that unity, ascend into the condition of the higher.

Causes of error in worship.
c. 21.

49. Having admitted fully that there are forms and modes of worship which do assume imperfection and passion in the gods, he lays down the important maxim that these have arisen from men attributing their own passions to the gods, instead of seeking the gods to deliver them from their passions. Hence all modes of adoration and sacrifice are justifiable upon the very ground upon which Porphyry would condemn them. They express " a venerable steadfastness, an intellectual joy, a wonder that cannot turn from its object, a fixed purpose of mind." Hence it becomes necessary to describe the orders and operations of the divine powers, that we may base our reverence and worship upon them. This is the subject of a large portion of the treatise. We can only seize a few particulars of this elaborate theogony and theophany, from which our readers may judge of the rest. The appearances of the gods are simple; those of the dæmons various: those of the angels more simple than these, but inferior to the purely divine; those of the archangels approaching nearer to those of the primary gods; those of the rulers of the world who direct elements very various and complex, though all marshalled in due order. Those who preside over matter still manifest themselves in greater varieties than these: souls in all manner of forms. The appearances of the gods are satisfactory

Section II.
cc. 8. 1—9.

to the vision; those of the archangels at once mild and awful but more gentle than those of the angels; those of the dæmons terrible. The appearances of heroes are more gentle than those of the dæmons; those of the rulers of the elements painful and grievous; those of souls like those of heroes, but weaker. It is impossible not to trace a Jewish element in these distinctions. The Rabbis have evidently conversed with the priest, as in Egypt they were likely enough to do. Something of the old Jewish feeling, that the Lord of All must not only be the mightiest, but the most gracious of all, is traceable through his refinements. The philosopher of course has also his own word to contribute to the exposition. What it is, Abammon will tell us presently.

50. He fully admits the assertion of Porphyry that knowledge of the gods is the highest of all blessings; ignorance the greatest curse. That, he says, is a commonplace in which all are agreed. Nor does he doubt that intellectual effort or meditation is a necessary condition of communion with the gods. But it is not the only condition; the philosopher, as such, may perceive the need of communion, but he does not attain it. Something else is required. Not tricks or deceptions inconsistent with philosophy, as Porphyry supposes. Truth does not proceed from our minds, but from the gods. Priests do not invent; they are the channels of communication. Hence we are introduced to the whole subject of divination. Fore-knowledge, we are told in the outset, is not physical, not artificial, not human,—altogether divine and supernatural, sent down from above. First of dreams. There is a divine dreaming, a state between sleeping and waking, in which divine voices are heard and divine visions perceived, which is to be wholly distinguished from the dreaming that is dependent upon bodily impressions and earthly recollections. The difference turns upon the great doctrine that souls have a two-fold relation,—one to the Divinity, one to the body. Next the divine afflatus is explained, and the test of it laid down. Those who have it have surrendered their whole lives as mere instruments and organs to the inspiring gods. They either obtain the divine life instead of their human life, or they waste their own life in obedience to the god. Such persons may touch fire and not be burnt; may be struck with axes and knives on their backs or arms and not perceive it. Their actions are no more human; they may trample on fire or walk through water. There are various forms of this inspiration: it may possess some of the limbs, or the whole body. Some are agitated; some are preternaturally quiet. The whole process of the divine enthusiasm is then described. It must not be called ecstasy, for it translates the mind to something higher,—not merely carries it away, it might be into a lower or more animal

Knowledge of the gods. § II. c. 11.

§ III. c. 1. Divination.

§ III. c. 2 & 3.

c. 4, s. 6, 7, 8.

state. The true enthusiasm does not come from soul or body: it is wholly divine. The man who has it is simply possessed by the gods. Porphyry had inquired into the effect of music in producing this enthusiasm. He is answered that sounds as such can have no influence in bringing about a state which is so entirely divine; that the sounds indicate that inner harmony which there is between the soul and the gods. In them it recognises this harmony, through them may ascend towards it, and so may be ready to receive the full inspiration. All the different agencies which have been connected with divination are to be accounted for upon this same principle. The vapour which the Delphic priestess inhales is not the inspiration of the god; but it is a symbol or instrument which the god may use for the purification of the man, and for fitting him to receive his divine gifts.

§ III. c. 9.

§ III. c. c. 10 & 11.

Causes of fore-knowledge.
51. We need not enumerate the number of inferences and applications of this doctrine into which Abammon enters: the one law being that all divination is directly and purely from the gods, the intermediate agencies are treated as entirely ministerial. Neither the birds, nor the entrails, nor the air, nor the prophet, nor the human soul itself, nor the soul considered as mixed of the human and the divine, nor any passion or affection of it, nor any disease or madness, can be its origin. The power of foretelling is not a natural instinct, such as belongs to animals; it has nothing in common with the foresight of the sailor or the physician; it is no effect of chance or magical art; it cannot be attributed to some sympathy between different bodies, so that we may talk of the seeds of prophecy being in us. Further, our author not only derides the notion that idols can be of any avail to the prophet, but he denounces them as worthless and mischievous; he declares that the human maker of the idols is himself better than all the works of his hands; he affirms that nothing which has been compounded by human art can be simple and pure; he declares that the divine light will not shine into the soul of the man who looks upon these as gods. Porphyry had hinted at the existence of evil and deceptive spirits. His opponent does not question their existence; bad men indulging evil passions draw such evil spirits through sympathy towards themselves. But the true priest is their great antagonist: so little does his inspiration proceed from them, that it arises from that submission of mind to the pure Being which puts all evil thoughts and tempers, and all evil spirits, to flight.

§ III. c. 11, —27.

cc. 28, 29, 30.

§ III. c. 31.

Defence of Providence.
52. The two principles which Abammon has put forward, that all prayer to the gods rests upon an internal affinity between them and their worshippers, and that all evils belong to the partial,

not to the universal, are further pressed in answer to Porphyry's awkward questions respecting the power which the inferior being appears to exert over the superior, and the moral evils which are ascribed to those who demand at least an outward purity from their ministers. On this last point our Egyptian theurgist stammers somewhat more than he is wont to do; he hints at the old and modern plea, that our justice and the justice of the gods may be different; that our partial laws cannot bind them; that they see into the heart of things, while we only see a little way, &c. &c. But, then feeling the inconsistency of these propositions with his main doctrine, he professes out of mere grace and courtesy to discard them, and returns to the maxim that nothing but what is good can originate from the gods; that their sublime and mysterious loves may be misinterpreted when they are looked at through the divided and partial lights of human judgment; and that the authors of corrupt and immoral acts, among men, must be the evil dæmons. § IV. c. 4.

c. 6 & 7.

53. In the next section Abamman enters at large upon the whole subject of sacrifice. The question, he admits, is a very great one, liable to errors on various sides. Sacrifices cannot be resolved into mere acts of adoration or thank-offerings, nor into certain necessary relations between the different portions of the world, which certainly exist but do not determine the acts and purposes of the gods, who are above nature. All supposed physical analogies between lower natures and the higher celestial natures, such as the animal worshippers of Egypt imagined, are discarded for the same reason. The origin of sacrifices must be drawn from the gods themselves, from a friendship and sympathy between the creators and the things created, the begetters and those who are begotten. The gods do not feed upon the matter of sacrifices; the fire burns that up. That fire is the counterpart of a divine fire, which has the effect of separating the corrupt elements in the man from the divine and celestial. (This meaning is certainly contained in the words, but, by a natural and sufficiently common process of thought, the material and immaterial fires become so blended in Abammon's discourse, that the distinction between them is not always perceptible to us, nor perhaps to himself.) The kinds of sacrifices are then shown to correspond to the different kinds of the Gods, to the character and state of the worshipper, to the threefold division of human life,—into the purely intellectual, the physical, and that which is compounded of both. Seeing that there is this proportion and relation, there must be a theurgic science to ascertain the number and orders of the gods, and the sacrifice which is appropriate to each. The greatest damage may accrue to man from leaving any one of Section V.

Sacrifice.

Section V. c. 1—10.

c. 11.

Forms of Sacrifice.

c. 18.

the superior beings unheeded, or not heeded in his own proper method. Then comes out the very essence of the whole Neo-Platonic divinity. Might not the sacrifices be better if they were directed to *the* one, and if in him all the various substances and powers were worshipped together? No doubt. But this possibility comes very late, and to a very, very few; a man may be glad enough if it happens to him at the end of his life. And since the universe is composed of a number of different orders, we must try by the number and variety of sacrifices to comprehend them all.

Worship of the One.
c. 22.

54. In the next section he defends the different usages of Egyptian worship, apologising for the threats which the theurgist uses as being directed to the inferior dæmons, who are entrusted with some of the secrets of the universe which they might reveal. They may be held in check by the terrors of the priestly authority, which is wielded in the name of the higher gods. The Egyptians, he intimates, whose worship is more addressed to the dæmons, occasionally introduce these threats into the higher worship. This is an error from which the Chaldæans, who address themselves more to the higher gods, are free. Abammon then enters upon an explanation of the Egyptian theosophy; affirms its general principle to be, that the gods delight in making all lower things typical of the higher; touches upon the Lotus and the Zodiac; defends the use of barbarous names rather than of Greek—the former being original and of divine institution, and especially dedicated to divine mysteries and communion—the latter having been altered according to human art and pleasure. Entering further into the belief of his countrymen, in reply to Porphyry's question respecting their notion of a primary cause, he declares the doctrine of Hermes to be, that, before all substances and the principalities of the world, there is one God, earlier than the first god and king, remaining unmoved in the singleness of his own unity. For neither is the intellectual interwoven with him nor anything else. He is his own archetype,—his own Father,—begotten from himself,—*the* good. For he is greatest and first, and fountain of all things, and root of all the intelligible forms......He is the beginning and the God of gods, a monad out of the one, the first substance and the beginning of substance. He is the ruler of the Noetic principalities which are the oldest of all, above the empyreal, and ætherial, and celestial. Next to this being comes Eicton, the first of the intelligences,—to be worshipped in silence: then Emeth, Ammon, Osiris, and so forth. Matter was produced by dividing the essence from that in which it inheres; or, as the author says, despising the obvious jokes of scoffers, by dividing materiality from essentiality. Hermes

Threats.
§ VI. c. 5.
c. 7.

Theosophy.
§ VII.
c. 1—5.

Sect. VIII.
1—6.

USE OF THIS TREATISE. 79

taught the Egyptians how to ascend from the natural and fatal to the divine. It is a mistake to say that they subject the human will to the movement of the stars; the gods are above fate, and men ascending to the gods partake of their freedom.

55. Touching for a while upon the astrological speculations of the Egyptians, Abammon denies that the dæmon who rules over a man's life and destiny is to be ascertained from any observation of the stars. The dæmon who rules in a man existed before the soul came down to birth,—he is present with the soul, he rules its proper life; all our thoughts have their origin from him; all we do he puts into our minds, and leads us on till by the help of the priestly theurgy we acquire a god instead of a dæmon as leader of our souls: then he gives place to one higher than himself. The writer concludes with asserting the high and pure motives of the theurgist. He finds man fallen from the vision of God,—he knows that he can only be blessed by recovering that vision: his whole business is to lead him up by gradual steps till he connects his spirit, freed from all matter, with the eternal word. The perfect good is God himself; the good of man is unity with him. Abammon prays the gods, for himself and correspondent, that they would grant them to hold fast all right thoughts; that they would infuse into them and keep within them the truth for ever; that they would vouchsafe them a more perfect participation of divine knowledge, wherein consists the blessed accomplishment of all other good things; and would grant them the enjoyment of sympathy and fellowship with each other.

The dæmon within.
§ IX. 1—9.

Concluding prayer.
§ X. c. 8.

56. Long as has been our report of this celebrated treatise, we believe we have saved our readers' time by our copious analysis of it. For it anticipates so much of all the arguments, good and evil, by which theurgy has been defended from that day to this; it is so very much abler than most of the imitations of it which have been produced in later times; the depth and truth of some of its principles serve so admirably to expose the abuse of them; that we shall have but to refer back to Abammon as having already told us all that can be told of the subject. The one question we have to consider, before we leave the third century and enter upon the more stirring subjects which present themselves to us in the fourth, is in what relation the Christian Church stood to this philosophico-theological party,—whether it had anything to do with the questions which were discussed between Porphyry and Abammon,—to which side of the controversy its weight must have inclined.

The views of the Church.

57. No one, we suppose, can doubt for an instant that the debate was one which concerned the Christian student most

deeply, or that he had many motives which must have drawn him each way. How gladly might he hail the keen and searching interrogations by which Porphyry seemed to lay bear the whole theory of polytheistic worship, making its hollowness evident! What a satisfaction to claim the skilful antagonist of the Church, as its witness against the Heathen world! But, on the other hand, how much of Abammon's doctrine coincided with the most sacred and precious portions of their own! How entirely he was at one with them, as to the end for which man lives and which he is to pursue! How well he had defended their own great principle that God himself is the author of all the good that comes to men; that the prayers and sacrifices which ascend to Him must themselves originate with Him! How clearly, too, he had asserted a direct affinity between God and His creatures, and had made this and not some external edict the foundation of worship! Surely such views had more of the Christian savour in them than the proud negative criticism of the mere philosopher.

56. Nor must it be concealed that the Christians of this age had another point of attraction to the school of Abammon and Iamblichus. The love of theurgy, or thaumaturgy, was as natural to them as to any other men in the empire. They believed that their Master had asserted his control over the powers of nature, and over the life of man. They believed that His followers were to do greater works than even He did upon earth. It was only at times that they could see that the startling and the prodigious did not belong to the essence of His works,—was scarcely an accident of them; that they were calm, regular, restorative, asserting God's control, and, in a subordinate sense, man's control over the influences and energies of nature; vindicating laws rather than producing exceptions. It was not to be expected that that which looked wonderful to a sensual, magic-ridden people, should not seem most wonderful to them, and the highest sign of Christ's dominion. Bitter experience was needful to prove how quickly such an apprehension might lead them back into the heart of the idolatry from which they believed that miracles and all other divine manifestations had been intended as the deliverance. Other aspects of the priestly doctrine closely connected with these, also would be welcomed with only too much readiness. Mutatis mutandis, Abammon had put forth more clever pleas for the honouring of relics, for the respect which was just beginning to be paid to local saints, for speculations about the angelic host and their relationship to men, than any refiner of their own could have supplied; a plea just as much qualified as theirs could have been by protests against vulgar, materialising idolatry. Where,

INADEQUACY OF THEORIES.

then, was their standing point? Might some of them be Porphyrians, and some of them Iamblichans? Or, did their faith hang in an uncertain balance between the two?

57. These who speak of Christianity as a religion, or a collection of dogmas, and of the Church as a set of doctors, will, if they are faithful to the facts, return the most various answers to these questions. Those who regard the Church in the light in which it presented itself to the Roman Emperors, and in which it was proclaimed by Christ himself and his apostles, as a kingdom, can understand why it was possible that its subjects should have been utterly unable to represent their position adequately in a theory, and should have exhibited in their writings many of the confusions which were incidental to all existing theories, yet should have maintained their ground and enlarged their borders in the midst of the most tremendous persecutions from without, and of their own imperfections and contradictions within. The root, it would seem, of Porphyry's inability to reach to Heaven by philosophy, the warrant for the theurgy of Abammon, and for the infinite superstitions which lay within it, was the same. If there was no one living person in whom the Creator and the creature met, one of these schemes was inevitable, neither could attain its result. If there was, the history of the world would shew, what Christian as little as Heathen teachers could shew, where the philosophical and theological methods really coincide, how impracticable and how useless to mankind are any artificial experiments for bringing them into harmony.

General conclusions.

CHAPTER III.

THE FOURTH CENTURY.

The new æra.

1. THE transition from the reign of Diocletian to the reign of Constantine strikes the ecclesiastical historian as the most violent in history. He speaks of the age of persecution as terminating in the age of patronage, the most violent and systematic effort ever made to exterminate a society in the acknowledgment of it to the exclusion of every other. The civil historian finds more points of resemblance between the periods; Diocletian had weakened the prestige of the ancient capital before Constantine established the new one. The forms of the Republic were already giving place to oriental habits and arrangements which were to be adopted and consecrated by the new faith in Byzantium. The historian of philosophy finds the later period evolving itself very naturally out of the previous one; yet no one is more compelled than he is to take notice of the great crisis which separates them.

Constantine how far a Neo-Platonist.

2. The Neo-Platonic philosophy has been called in of late years to explain some phenomena in the life of the first Christian Emperor. It may serve that purpose if we are careful to recollect that Constantine was a Roman and not a Greek, a soldier and not a sophist. Whatever influence he received from the schools, came to him changed and transformed by the world's atmosphere. He probably believed, as the teachers of the new sect believed, that there was a supreme and universal God; he believed that that supreme God had subordinate gods and dæmons through whom his power was exercised, his existence and character manifested to men. But there is no reason to suppose that he had ever formally embraced these tenets, or that he knew that they were maintained by any celebrated teachers, or that he had remoulded his traditional Paganism in conformity with them. They were in all probability the common, prevalent notions among men of ordinary education, who were capable of receiving the impressions of the age to which they belonged, and who, without comparing them or reducing them into system, had eyes open to read the commentaries upon them which experience supplied. The old forms, simply as forms, had lost their hold upon men of this character. Galerius or Maxi-

mianus might uphold them as part of the military code which it was a breach of discipline to transgress; Diocletian might support them as an imperial theory: but a young man bred under the moderate and liberal Constantius, observing the failure of their experiments though made on so large a scale, and on the whole with so much skill, might, even if his personal feelings had not been disgusted, have arrived gradually at the conclusion that they were pledged to a hopeless cause. Yet no *doctrine*, we may be sure, could ever commend itself to his mind as having a special claim upon his devotion and sympathy; he never could have exchanged that belief which was bound up with the history of his country and of the world, for the most reasonable theosophy or dæmonology. He was only discontented with that belief because it was evidently weak, too weak to uphold a polity such as Rome ought to be; he tried it by such a standard, not because he was insincere, or regarded religious sanctions as the inventions of priests or sages, but because he had no other proof that they were more than this, that they were fixed and divine, except so far as they sufficed for the political end. *To be judged as an ordinary Roman.*

3. To suppose all these processes for a long time at work in his mind, is not to pronounce an opinion whether he actually saw the vision which he spoke of in his later years, on the eve of his battle with Maxentius; far less is it to suggest the thought that he did not really arrive at the conclusion that the cross was the sign in which he must conquer, or that he was not led to that conclusion by the highest of all teachers. What we wish to intimate is, that the conviction, however suddenly brought home in its full power to Constantine—and it may be quite consistent with reason and experience that there should have been a critical moment which decided his whole after-course—that the eagle must stoop to the symbol of ignominy and crime, had been working itself out in the mind of a man, by all the experiences of his life, and in the mind of a people by the experiences of several generations. What we would wish Christians, and those who are not Christians, equally to consider, is whether all such thoughts, and the circumstances which suggested them, do not more imply a spiritual guide of man, and one who uses events for man's education, than the apparition of the Labarum, were it authenticated by the most absolute evidence, could possibly do. *His conversion gradual.*

4. Henceforth, then, that polity which confessed a moral and metaphysical basis—which affirmed that there was a supernatural Will and a righteous Will, who was holding its members together and binding them into one—was acknowledged by the polity which seemed to rest on a mere arbitrary and earthly will, as necessarily yoked with it, as in some sense its superior. The Empire which could not gratify the modest ambition of Plotinus *The Church and the Empire in their union.*

by allowing him to set up a Platonopolis in Campania, had deliberately conceded to a set of men whom they had persecuted perseveringly for ten years, and at intervals for two hundred, the right of establishing *their* city in every province of the Empire; of reorganising the institutions of Rome, and of introducing their own at its very outset into the new Constantinople. The blow to the tottering idols of the east and west was tremendous; but it was scarcely a less severe blow to the rising philosophy. For Ammonius, if not a deserter from the Christian ranks, had at least hoped that his occult philosophy would have undermined its broad and popular statements: Plotinus had substituted the ascent of the divine man into the original and absolute divinity, for the idea of the Son of God stooping to take Man's nature. Porphyry had felt and expressed the opposition which was latent in his master; Iamblichus, and the school most opposed to Porphyry, were deliberately trying to resuscitate Polytheism, and to make its notions of divine descents into earthly natures harmonise with the Greek wisdom, which they said had originally been borrowed from the Egyptian Hermes. By the middle of Constantine's reign, Licinius had gathered together some of the ruder elements of Paganism, and had engaged them in a religious war. But it needed some other head to associate polytheism, Greek philosophy, the dream of old Roman glory, in one valiant effort against the new faith: nor could such a person appear till that faith had already been mightily shaken from within, and till some of the strange effects of the union of the Empire and the Church had made themselves apparent.

Its effects on the Platonic school.

Connection of the Arian controversy with philosophy.

5. The Arian controversy, which affected so seriously the civil condition of the Empire, is no less involved with the history of philosophy. We have seen how much all questions of this time turned upon the relation between the highest being and some power or powers at some distance below him, more nearly related to man. The faith of Constantine had probably assigned some indistinct place of this kind to Him whom he nevertheless had acknowledged as supreme over himself and the Roman world. When Arius, in language not very intelligible to the Emperor, affirmed the inferiority of Christ to the Father of All, he could feel no serious objection to the statement, though he was anxious that the subject should not be stirred. When the earnestness of the combatants made his mode of reconciliation ineffectual, he wisely appealed to a council, and enforced its decrees though they asserted the consubstantiality of the Son with the Father. But he repented of that course when he perceived that the dispute was not at rest, and readily embraced the dexterous suggestion of Eusebius, so well fitted for the temper

of the monarch, and indicating such an accurate judgment of the desire for quiet in the better sort of the Clergy—of promotion in the worse—that the addition of a single iota to the formula would satisfy the minds of all reasonable people. Athanasius had courage to resist that proposition, believing that it involved nothing less than the inroad of all the Neo-Platonic dæmonology and with that, of all Heathenism; believing that the church stood as a Society and a Kingdom upon the acknowledgment of a person in whom the Godhead and Manhood were actually reconciled. The Emperor and his son Constantius treated him as an enemy and as the disturber of the world. A majority of the Eastern Bishops agreed with them, and Semi-Arianism triumphed in the palace of the Cæsars and in the councils of the Church—every where except in the deserts of the Thebais and amidst some, not all, the Bishops of the West—till the time of Julian.

Feelings of Athanasius.

6. That young man had enough of reason for hating the memory of his uncle, and the acts of his cousin; enough of excuse for regarding the prelates of Constantinople with contempt. He might have dreamed, he probably did dream, while he was yet in the court where his nearest relations had been murdered, that the days of the older Cæsars would return, if the faith which they professed returned also. He might have the most plausible reasons for thinking that the house which seemed to him to stand on such a new and feeble foundation, would *not* stand now that it was divided against itself. Athens was needed to ripen these thoughts into maturity; Julian had enough of knowledge to recall something of its ancient greatness,—enough of imagination to feel that that glory was not departed while there were still philosophers to teach in its gardens. These philosophers opened to him the Neo-Platonic mysteries; mixed with them lay the brilliant forms of the old Mythology, which they could again bring to light. His strength might have evaporated in these visions; his commission to Gaul, and his campaign there, made him conscious of more active powers, and shewed him that he was qualified to rule an army or a people. The three conditions which were necessary for the representative and champion of the world that had fallen, met in him. He entered all armed with the sympathies of a great multitude, with the abilities of a man of letters, and with the command of an Empire, upon the task which he had assigned himself.

Education of Julian.

7. Julian lived only thirty-three years, and reigned only two. But a great part of the thought and mind of his age is expressed in that brief life. The experiment which philosophers had been making in their closets, and continued to make for two centuries, began to be tried on a scale commensurate with

Importance of his history.

its importance, when he arrived at Constantinople and found himself in possession of the empire; was terminated when he fell in Persia. No one has ever questioned his ability, the steadiness of his purpose, or the greatness of his zeal. He had too full a share of prudence. He concealed his attachment to the old gods till he could assist effectually in re-establishing their worship. His measures for that purpose had all the air of being tolerant measures, while yet they effectually crippled the Christians, and would soon have deprived them of what was infinitely more precious than court patronage,—the means of obtaining education. What is important for our purpose is, that Julian fancied himself primarily a philosopher, that his devotion to the Sun, and Minerva, and Serapis, seemed to him a part of his philosophy; that he valued his imperial position mainly because it enabled him to do the work which he supposed was demanded by philosophy. Jovian, who followed him, was simply a soldier. Valens, his successor in the East, was a theological dogmatist; Valentinian, a Roman, who looked upon Christian orthodoxy in the way Decius and Aurelian had looked upon Pagan orthodoxy, as that which it behoved well-disciplined soldiers to uphold. Theodosius, something in the same spirit, but with a character of greater breadth formed in a school of suffering, deliberately trampled upon Arianism with one foot and on Paganism with the other, leaving the first, when it could no longer rule in the palace of the Cæsars, to find a home among the Gothic tribes; the other, when its Greek, Egyptian, Italian temples were overthrown, to intrench itself secretly and securely in the heart of the Catholic church. The miserable reigns of Arcadius and Honorius link this century to the one which saw the downfall of the western empire.

8. There are many names in this century which are dear to the ecclesiastical biographer; a few on which the ordinary annalist may dwell. There are three men whom the student of philosophy must pause to contemplate,—the two we have mentioned already, Athanasius and Julian, the third, Augustine. The theologian may consider this last thinker under the fifth century, which contains the period of his episcopacy, and of his battles with Donatists and Pelagians. But the time in which his mind was formed, the Manichæan portion of his history, is the one in which we are mainly interested. We shall endeavour to give our readers just so many extracts from the writings of each of these men as may explain why we introduce them, and how we suppose they illustrate their time.

9. In the oration against the Gentiles, Athanasius speaks thus:—In the beginning Evil was not, even as now it is not in

ORIGIN OF EVIL.

the saints, nor hath any substantial existence in respect of them. But afterwards men conceived it, and, to their own injury, put it into forms. Wherefore also they conceived the notion of idols, counting the things that are not as though they were. For God, the Former of all, and the universal King, He that transcends all substance and human knowledge, being good and superlatively excellent, by His own Word our Saviour Jesus Christ made the human race in His own image, and fitted him (man,) through this likeness to behold and take cognizance of the things which are; giving him also the perception and knowledge of his own eternity; that preserving this resemblance (or identity, τὴν ταυτότητα) he might never at any time withdraw from the vision of God, nor depart from the fellowship of the saints; but holding fast the grace of Him that bestowed it, and that proper power which he received from the Word of the Father, he might rejoice in the Divinity, and hold converse with Him, living a harmless and truly blessed and immortal life. For having nothing to hinder his knowledge of the Godhead, he beholds always through his own purity the image of the Father in whose image he was made. And he wonders as he contemplates the providence over the universe, which comes through Him, being made far above the sensible things and all bodily phantasy in contact through his noetic faculty with the divine and noetic things. For when the reason of men doth not converse with bodies, then hath it not any mixture of the desire which comes from these, but is wholly at one with itself, as it was from the beginning. Then passing through sensible and human things, it becomes raised up, and beholding the Word, sees in Him also the Father of the Word, delights itself with the contemplation of Him, continually renews itself afresh with the longing after Him; even as the Holy Scriptures say that man (who in the Hebrew tongue was called Adam), with unashamed boldness maintained his mind towards God, and had intercourse with the saints in that contemplation of noetic things which he held in the place figuratively named by Moses Paradise. For the purity of the soul is such that through it one may even see God; as our Lord says, in his beatitudes. Well, the Architect thus prepared man, and wished him thus to remain. But men having despised the nobler substances, and having become wearied of pursuing these, sought rather for those that were nearer to themselves. The nearer things were the body and its sensations; whereby men withdrew their reason from noetic things; contemplating themselves and occupying themselves with the body and other sensible objects: beguiled as it were in that which was their own, they fell into the love of themselves, preferring that which was theirs to the contemplation of that which is God's. And

Proper condition of man.

Man's connection with the spiritual world.

Declension.

THE FALL OF MAN INTO THE SENSIBLE.

having become thoroughly engaged with these, and not being willing to withdraw from those things which were close at hand, they shut up in the pleasures of the body their soul, which was disturbed and confused with all manner of lusts. At last they forgot altogether that faculty of theirs which they had from God. And this truth one might see from that which the Holy Scriptures speak concerning the first man that was formed. For he who had his mind towards God, and the contemplation of Him, withheld himself from that contemplation which turns downwards towards the body. But when, through the counsel of the serpent, he withdrew from that reason which looks towards God, and began to take account of himself, straightway he and his wife fell into the lust of the body, and knew that they were naked, and in consequence of that knowledge were ashamed. They knew themselves naked, not so much of clothes, but that they had become naked of the vision of divine things, and had turned their mind toward that which was contrary to these. When they had apostatized from that knowledge which has respect to the one and the living Being, I mean God, and from the love which is towards Him, they rushed thenceforth into the divided and partial lusts of the body. Then, as is wont to happen, having embraced the desire of each thing, and of many things, they began to be so bound and fastened to these, that they feared to let them go. Hence there came to the soul cowardly anticipations and terrors, and all thoughts that savour of mortality. For not wishing to part with its desires, it fears death and the separation from the body. And coveting again and not being able to obtain things answering to its desires, it learnt violence and murder. How it doth these things it may be right as far as we can to explain. Having revolted from the contemplation of noetic things, misusing the partial energies of the body, pleased with the contemplation, and fancying pleasure to be good for it, it abuses in its confusion that name of the good, and thinks pleasure to be the actual good. Just as a madman asks for a sword to strike every one he meets with, and convinces himself that he is playing the part of a wise man. And being enamoured of pleasure, the soul began to use its energies in various ways. For being by nature quick and free of movement, it must retain this quality even after it has withdrawn from the good; only it is moved no longer according to virtue nor so as to see God, but prizing the things that are not, having free-will either to turn to the good or to turn away from it, it misuses all the power which belongs to it for the gratification of those lusts which it has conceived. And it finds in virtue of this free will that it can direct the different portions of its body both ways, either to the things that are or the things that are not. The things that are, are the good, inasmuch as they are

The complete Fall.

The consequences of Evil to the man.

Pleasure becomes the good.

OBJECTS OF ATHANASIUS.

the likenesses of the God who is. The things that are not, I call the evil things, inasmuch as they have been fashioned by the thoughts of men." Athanasius then proceeds to point out how each member and energy of the body is turned away from the special good for which it was formed, and to the evil which is the perversion of it, winding up with the words: "All which things are the soul's corruption and sin. But of these there is no other cause save the revolt from the higher and better things. As if a charioteer should be utterly careless of the goal towards which it behoves him to drive; should merely urge the horses just as he can (and where he can, means where he likes); and so ofttimes he falls foul of those who meet with him; oft-times he is carried down precipices, whither by help of the swiftness of the horses he has conveyed himself, all the time not thinking that he has erred from his aim; he looks only to the chariot." Then, after quoting the passage from St. Paul, respecting the prize of his high calling, he adds: "Certain of the Greeks having wandered from the right way, and not having known the Christ, have affirmed evil to be in substance, and to have an actual existence of its own, grounding this opinion upon one of two errors. Either they deny the Demiurgus to be the creator of the things that are, or they say, because He is the creator of the universe He must needs be the creator of evil. For evil, according to them, is among the things that are. But the evil does not come out of the good, nor is it in it, nor is it through it. For that would not be good which had a mixed nature, or which was the cause of evil. The heretics, too, who have fallen from the Church's teaching, and have made shipwreck of faith, they also fancy evil to have a substance. And they feign to themselves another God besides the true Father of the Christ, and make him the unbegotten author of evil, the introducer of mischief, the Demiurgus of the creation." These he proceeds to confute from the Scriptures.

_{Ground of the notion that Evil is part of creation.}

10. Much we think is to be learnt from this extract respecting the character and purpose of its author, and also respecting the movements of his time. Many who have only heard of Athanasius as a theologian, or who have heard that he had far less of intellectual training than other churchmen of the century, such as Basil and Gregory, or who rightly conceive of him as a man mainly remarkable for energetic action and that power of writing letters on business for which Gibbon gives him abundant credit, will be surprised to find how much of the Alexandrian habit of thought belongs to him, how naturally he uses the philosophical dialect, how much there is to connect a work so professedly Christian and polemical as this with those which are ostentatiously Platonic. Even the specimen we have given will prevent them

_{Athanasius a philosopher.}

90   THE BATTLE OF THE CHURCH AND PAGANISM.

<small>Connection of his philosophy with his practical objects.</small>
from supposing that these characteristics are owing to any propensity which Athanasius had for heathen teachers, from any want of readiness to follow Tertullian in connecting the heretics of the Church with them. It was for the most thoroughly practical purpose that he betook himself to what some of our later divines and ecclesiastical historians delight to call 'mystical refinements.' He found that idolatry, the whole scheme of outward and sensual worship, could only be resisted by a decided pertinacious assertion that man is a spiritual being, and in that character has a distinct relation to a spiritual author and a spiritual object. Had he disowned what is called Mysticism, merely regarding the Scriptures as the revelation of an outward economy, of certain doctrines to be held, of certain precepts to be followed, the magnificent outward economy of the Roman empire, the doctrines so subtle and ingenious—touching human experience on so many sides—of the new philosophical school, the various precepts for good or evil which had descended as heir-looms from the past, or were struck out by sage moderns, would certainly have prevailed. It was only if he could show that what he held to be a revelation from God actually discovered the true constitution of Man; only if he could show that it was by resisting and breaking loose from this constitution that men had become disorderly, evil, idolatrous; only if he could show that the Christian economy or church involved the recognition of this true constitution, and was based upon it, and that any world-system, however compact and coherent, which assumed any other basis, which rested upon the worship of visible things, and derived its sanction from that worship, must be rotten and inhuman,—only then could he hope that Paganism would really fall, by whatsoever powers, visible or invisible, it might be upheld. How well founded the conclusion was, we think is made sufficiently clear by the writings which interpret the acts, and the acts which interpret the writings of the Emperor Julian.

<small>His life a stuggle against Idolatry.</small>

<small>Lost books.</small>   11. It seems to us that in general too many lamentations are wasted over lost books. Without attempting to controvert the extravagant conceit of Bacon—that only the lightest treasures have floated down the stream of time while the heaviest have sunk—by maintaining the opposite doctrine, which might be equally unreasonable, we may question whether chasms in books of history have not awakened a diligence and spirit of investigation for which the lost documents would have been a very feeble compensation, whether the books of poetry which have disappeared might not rather have disturbed than completed our image of the artist from whom they came. We certainly have no such transcendant opinion of Julian's writings as to make

him an exception from this remark, and to wish very earnestly that certain lost volumes which the industry of Christian divines is said to have suppressed, should have survived. And yet that act, however well intended, seems to us so exceedingly faithless, and has evidently left such a strange suspicion on many minds of something having been uttered by him which was especially profound and dangerous, that we may confess a stronger temptation to regret this act of violence than many others which have deprived us of possessions more intrinsically valuable. It might have been exceedingly instructive to have every possible help for ascertaining the habit and course of thinking in such a man. It might have enabled us to understand much better wherein lay the weakness of that society which he was seeking to undermine; what that strength was which prevailed against him. *The books of Julian against Christianity. Folly of those who destroyed them.*

12. The books which remain to us may, however, be sufficient for our purpose. Nothing can exceed the vehement affection with which Julian, in his epistles, addresses his philosophical friends. Libanius is always his "most sweet and beloved brother." On receiving one of his orations, he falls into a rapture. "What a style! What composition! What divisions! What arguments! What order! What harmony!" &c. He implores Aristomenes to come to him; for though he has never seen his face, he loves him, and wants him to show in Cappadocia what a true Greek is. He reads over the letters of Maximus as Alexander went to sleep with the poems of Homer under his pillow. He entreats him with the profoundest humility to take his writings under his care, not because he is sure they are worth any thing, but because, like an old eagle, he may carry up the unfledged eaglets into the air, that the rays of the sun may ascertain whether they are genuine or bastard. Just at the time when he has been proclaimed Emperor by the legions in Gaul, he writes to the same friend expressing the intense anxiety he has felt for him, and calls Jupiter and the Sun to witness how he invoked them (not openly, for that would not have been safe), to know whether there were any calamities likely to befall him. Now, he tells him, he publicly and openly worships the gods—intimating clearly that he owed to Maximus some of his strongest impulses to this service, and that he looked upon the obligation as the greatest which any man could incur. But his profoundest admiration is reserved for Iamblichus. As soon as he saw a man who he supposed was bringing letters from the philosopher, he says he leapt up, embraced him, and wept for joy. When he had the letters themselves, he kissed them, put them to his eyes, held them fast, for fear lest the image of his countenance should depart while he was reading *Letters of Julian to Libanius. To Maximus To Iamblichus.*

92 JULIAN NOT NATURALLY A PHILOSOPHER.

the lines. He tells him that not only Pindar and Democritus and old Orpheus, but the whole body of Greeks who have attained to the height of philosophy, have been brought by him into the most perfect musical symphony; that he has the hundred eyes of Argus to guard the pure form of virtue, that his wisdom can take all the various forms which Proteus assumed; but that instead of hiding himself like Proteus, he sends forth rays of light like the sun which illuminates those near and those afar off.

These professions not dishonest.

13. These rhapsodies we firmly believe to be honest. Extravagant as they sound, they are not unnatural in a young man escaping from teachers whom he utterly loathed, and whose gross inconsistencies and worldliness offered great excuse for his dislike; to men who told him things which sounded most wonderful, and carried with them an air of demonstration, who led him into what seemed to him a newer and freer world, yet one which he recognised as the old world wherein his fathers had dwelt. Most of us have been too familiar with emotions not very dissimilar—the result, alas! of causes not at all dissimilar—in men of our own time, to be incredulous when we hear words of this kind from an enthusiast of the fourth century. But while we regard these utterances as in themselves sincere, we do not believe that they belong to the sincerest part of Julian's mind. He is evidently gazing at philosophy as a distant prodigy with which naturally he has very little to do, and which overawes him because he cannot approach it or closely grapple with it. It would be as unjust to compare him with Caliban, as to compare Maximus or Libanius with Trinculo; yet his prostrations and exclamations at the taste of the liquor they present to him, make us feel that it was as strange to the lips of the imperial youth as the wine was to the savage. It was not, however, for its own sake chiefly that he delighted in it. His clever, lively, and instructive book on the festival of the Cæsars, explains to what use he believed it might be turned; how seriously he hoped that the doctrines of the Pagan sage would save the empire which he thought that the Church was destroying, which he had good right to think that it would not be permitted to save.

Their extravagance accounted for.

Julian's Cæsars.

14. The Cæsars of Julian were written during the Saturnalia. He is not given to joke, he says, but since he wishes to preserve the rites of that season, he will try to compose something which shall be profitable without being too grave. He fulfils his promise. His humour, though not rich or various, is easy and pleasant. The different Cæsars of the old time are invited to a feast with the gods—Quirinus and Hercules introducing them. Some two or three are rejected as too odious even for the lowest

Purpose and method of the book.

THE DIFFERENT CÆSARS. 93

places at such a repast; the others are enccuraged to produce their different merits, that the gods may judge between them. Silenus sits by, acting the licensed fool at the divine court, and suggesting various topics of accusation against the past lives of the Emperors. By special favour, Alexander is allowed to appear, that Greece may have its own representative. The acts of the candidates are first proclaimed, Silenus always reminding them of some that had escaped their memory. But the gods observe that acts may be owing in a great degree to fortune; the purpose of the actors is far more important. Alexander is asked what he thought the most excellent of all things, and to what intent he worked and suffered. "That he might bring all things into subjection," he answers. Mercury asks him whether he thinks he succeeded. Alexander believes he did. "Ah! no," says Silenus, "my daughters, the grapes, conquered you." Alexander being well skilled in Aristotelian logic, replies that his battle was not with inanimate things, but with the race of beasts and men. "Consummate dialectician! in which class do you place yourself," enquires the scoffer. "Are you one of the inanimate things? For you were beaten continually by yourself, by your own anger or grief." "I was not thinking about myself," says Alexander. "When you talk of conquering yourself, you use an equivocal expression." "Capital logic again!" cries Silenus; "but that Indian who wounded you, had not he the better of you?" "Stop," cries Dionysus, seeing that Alexander is becoming furious, "or he will deal with you as he did with Clitus." Upon which Alexander is so abashed that he retires from the contest. Each of the Romans gives an answer different from that of Alexander, but in the same spirit: a slight cross-examination demolishes it. No one comes off so badly as Constantine. His highest ambition, according to Julian, was to get many things to himself, then to give many things away; ministering first to his own lusts, then to those of his friends. But when Marcus Aurelius was called he answers that the purpose of his life was to imitate the gods. He is asked what that imitation consisted in. He answers, "to want as few things for himself as possible, and to do as much good as possible to the greatest number." Silenus raises the usual objections; valid ones on the ground of his indulgence of Faustina and Commodus, which Marcus rather sophistically takes off. Another, on his little care for his own body, he affirms to be part of his imitation of the gods.

15. We have given a summary of Julian's best work, not only for the sake of doing him justice, but because it throws a light upon his scheme of life. Marcus was to be his model. *He* had sought to preserve the Empire by exalting philosophy

The seekers of fame discredited.

Conquest of self.

Character of Constantine.

Julian's hero Marcus Aurelius.

His maxims of life.

How Julian hoped to imitate him.

94   JULIAN'S PRIVILEGE.

against Christianity; Julian would make the same experiment. He had motives of indignation which Marcus had not. He had seen Christians tried in a new position, and had reason to know how large a portion had disgraced themselves in the trial. Iamblichus and Maximus were greater than any of the stoics who surrounded Marcus. Besides, they had been proved in this very conflict. The new Platonism had come forth expressly to *Hopes from* resist and supersede Christianity. It had not triumphed yet. *new Platonism.* But then how little encouragement it had received from those Pagan emperors who were most earnest to put down the church; how it had been frowned upon by the recent protectors of the church! What might it not do if it were only supported by *Julian's* one who was ready to carry out its precepts even more *indifference to bodily* thoroughly than Marcus had carried out the precepts of *decencies.* stoicism; who, instead of craving for the indulgences which *See his Misopogon,* Christian monarchs had thought necessary, was as indifferent to *p. 39, Ed. Paris, 1583.* food, sleep, cleanliness, as any Christian monk could possibly be; who detested the theatres and the circus as much as any one of the Galileans; who could adopt those charitable practices which had made them so much reverenced in the days of their poverty; who could reform the heathen priesthood upon the model of their austerer men.

Julian's love of nature. 16. But though this political end was, we apprehend, predominant in Julian's mind over any passion for philosophy merely as such, we should be wrong to overlook another tendency which is apparent in all his writings. The most genuine *See the passage in the Misopogon beginning ἐτύγχανον ἐγὼ χειμάζων παρὰ τὴν φίλην Λευκετιαν, κ.τ.λ.* and most pleasant passages in his letters, as well as in his more formal treatises, are certainly those which refer to outward nature. When he speaks of a beautiful country or a pleasant climate (like that of his dear Paris, though this city he loved also for the contrast which its rude Celtic inhabitants afforded to the gay theatre-loving citizens of Antioch) he seems to forget himself more than at any other time, and to be more carried away by the recollection of sounds and sights, and by his own emotions. One of his longest letters is about the growth and *The letter to Sarapion, p. 200, Ed. Paris.* beauty of the fig-tree, and any topic of the kind has evidently far more true charm for him than the noetic speculations in which he fancied that he took so great an interest. A considerable part of his affection for the old idolatry seems to have arisen *Not a taste cultivated in the Christian Church.* from this cause. It was a gratification of that admiration for visible things which the teaching in the Christian schools may very possibly have chilled rather than cultivated. Though there are traces in the letters of Basil, and Gregory of Nazianzum, of the same feeling, for their education had been in many respects similar—Athens had been a foster-mother to all three—yet in general the metaphysics of the divines of that century would seem to one very ardent in his sympathies with nature, cold and repellent. We may well conceive, if other counteracting influences were not strong, how ardently he would rush into a worship which clothed all outward powers and objects with that divinity which the Christians claimed for the invisible Father, the only-begotten Word, and the Divine Spirit.

17. Great evidence for this observation is to be found in Julian's "Hymn to the Sun." A considerable part of that celebrated composition, in which the author talks of the noetic and spiritual principles, the primary good, and so forth, is merely adopted from his teachers, as the "Essay on Man" was adopted from Bolingbroke. The part which is really his own is that wherein he tells us that there had been in him, from childhood upwards, an intense love of the eyes of this god, and that he had been raised up in his mind towards that ethereal light, and had longed to look steadily at it, and that all the beauties of the heavens had had an attraction for him, so that on a cloudless and clear night he became wholly occupied and absorbed, and could not understand what any one spoke to him or did to him; for which reason he was mistaken for a beardless astrologer, though he declares that no book of astrology had ever come into his hands, nor did he know what manner of thing it was. All these signs, he says, made him a follower and worshipper of the sun before he knew any thing about philosophy. Afterwards he presented himself to him as the glorious visible light in which all the intellectual and invisible was represented. *His Hymn to the Sun. Its philosophy. Introd. to the Hymn, p. 23, Ed. Paris, 1583.*

18. If the reader compares this last statement with the doctrine of Athanasius concerning the Light of Light, the very God of very God, he will, we think, have a key to the nature of Julian's idolatry, and indeed of all the philosophical idolatry of this century. The outward luminous object took the place of the Person in whom the Christian creed affirmed that the full divine glory was gathered up and manifested; the image to the eye was exchanged for the divine image of the invisible Father. The whole conflict was here. Julian perceived most clearly and rightly that it lay more between himself and Athanasius than between any other two men; that no earthly antagonist stood as much in the way of the restoration of the natural worship which he loved as the Bishop of Alexandria. And hence, we understand, too, the other cardinal difference between these two men,—a difference inseparably involved with this, which the extract we chose from Athanasius disclosed. While it would be exceedingly wrong to deny to Julian the honour of putting down many abuses and corruptions in the court of Constantinople, and in the empire generally, which Christian Cæsars to their shame had tolerated, it is equally impossible not to see *The teaching of Athanasius. How related to these feelings of Julian's. Julian's ignorance of the conflict with evil.*

96   AUGUSTIN.

Transition St. Augustin that Evil never presented itself to his mind in its own nature and tenor, as something cleaving close to man, and from which he needs emancipation. The goodness, therefore, which Julian adored in the gods was not a power to which he fled from an enemy that was assaulting his own being. The gods were general divinities to whom he paid a homage which satisfied partly certain devout instincts of his own mind, partly the traditions of old Rome, partly his Athenian culture, partly his dislike of the faith which his uncle and his cousin had professed. On such foundations the edifice which had been thrown down was to be rebuilt. That on such a foundation nothing can stand—that the grounds of every faith, polity, philosophy, must be laid in the acknowledgment of a conflict between good and evil, and on the eternity and victory of the former—the life of the next man of whom we have to speak, illustrating as it does the experience of that age, and of many after ages, we think will sufficiently demonstrate.

Carthage. 19. When last we heard of Carthage and the African Church, it was in contrast with Alexandria. The Christian hatred of philosophy and love of law and rhetoric were represented in the person of Tertullian. The education of Augustin might have fitted him to be as much of a rhetorician as his eminent countryman; there were many qualities of his mind which such a discipline would be likely to call forth. If he became one of the class which Tertullian dreaded, it was not because his father was a heathen, or because he remained so long out of the bounds of the Church; still less was it because he received any extraneous Greek culture. If he did not take up philosophy for the sake of Christianity, he owed his Christianity in a great measure to his philosophy. And he was most thoroughly a Latin, attaining to Greek books, it would seem, chiefly through translations; his language and modes of thought belonging strictly to the West.

Augustin without Greek culture.

20. Of no one can it be so truly said as of Augustin, that he received his lore from within and not from without,—that all his knowledge was purchased by the fiercest personal struggles. Whether he resorted to the Manichees, or to Plato, or to the Bible, it was that he might find an interpretation of himself. He had no doubt a craving, felt in his youth and never lost, for a very definite system of opinions. But the influences which *Driven from systems.* crossed this desire and drove him in search of another object were really the blessed influences of his life, those to which he owed all the strength of his own belief and all his power of teaching others. When he had got his system nearly complete under the voice which asked him, "What art thou?" and forced him in the heights or in the depths to find an answer to the

question, broke the thread of his speculations and forced him to begin anew. The oftener in his after life he heard that voice, and believed that it was the one which he was to make others hear, the more fresh and living and full of instruction for all ages did his words become. When he forgot it, and sought to build earthly tabernacles for Moses and Elias and his Divine Lord, his spirit became confused, and he forged afresh for mankind some of those very chains from which he had been set free.

21. "The Confessions," though not the book to which any one would turn for the formal philosophy of Augustin, is really the key to it all. The book must be studied throughout, if we would understand those portions of it which bear directly upon our own subject: indeed, its whole meaning is lost if we suppose that the passages in it which concern philosophy are not as intimately connected with Augustin himself, as those which describe his first joyful discernment of the meaning of the New Testament: he never separates them himself. Our extracts will illustrate this remark, and may help the reader to appreciate the real significance of a book which is much read, but little known. The following passage is from the third book; it refers to the time when he was in the rhetorical school of Carthage, where he was surrounded by a reckless band of libertines:— *Philosophy of the Confessions.*

22. "Among such as these, in that unsettled age of mine, learned I books of eloquence, wherein I desired to be eminent, out of a damnable and vain-glorious end, a joy in human vanity. In the ordinary course of study I fell upon a certain book of Cicero, whose speech almost all admire; not so his heart. This book of his contains an exhortation to philosophy, and is called '*Hortensius.*' But this book altered my affections, and turned my prayers to Thyself, O Lord; and made me have other purposes and desires. Every vain hope at once became worthless to me; and I longed with an incredibly burning desire for an immortality of wisdom, and began now to arise, that I might return to Thee. For not to sharpen my tongue, (which thing I seemed to be purchasing with my mother's allowances, in that my nineteenth year, my father being dead two years before), not to sharpen my tongue did I employ that book; nor did it infuse into me its style, but its matter. *Cicero's Hortensius.*

"How did I burn then, my God, how did I burn to re-mount from earthly things to Thee; nor knew I what Thou wouldest do with me. For with Thee is wisdom. But the love of wisdom is in Greek called 'philosophy,' with which that book inflamed me. Some there be that seduce through philosophy, under a great, and smooth, and honourable name colouring and disguising their own errors: and almost all who *Cicero a divine Teacher.*

in that and former ages were such, are in that book censured and set forth: there also is made plain that wholesome advice of Thy Spirit, by Thy good and devout servant; *Beware lest any man spoil you through philosophy and vain deceit, after the tradition of men, after the rudiments of the world, and not after Christ. For in him dwelleth all the fulness of the Godhead bodily.* And since at that time (Thou, O light of my heart, knowest) Apostolic Scripture was not known to me, I was delighted with that exhortation, so far only, that I was thereby strongly roused, and kindled, and inflamed to love, and seek, and obtain, and hold, and embrace not this or that sect, but wisdom itself whatever it were; and this alone checked me, thus enkindled, that the name of Christ was not in it.

22. The following passages from the 4th Book illustrate an important stage in his experience, and introduce us to his earliest work.

<small>The Beautiful.</small> "These things I then knew not, and I loved these lower beauties, and I was sinking to the very depths, and to my friends I said, 'do we love anything but the beautiful? What then is the beautiful? and what is beauty? What is it that attracts and wins us to the things that we love? for unless there were in them a grace and beauty, they could by no means draw us unto them.' And I marked and perceived that in bodies themselves, there was a beauty, from their forming a sort of whole, and again, another from apt and mutual correspondence, as of a part of the body with its whole, or a shoe with a foot, and the like. And this consideration sprang up in my mind, out of my inmost heart, and I wrote 'on the fair and fit,' I think two or three books. Thou knowest, O Lord, for it is gone from me; for I have them not, but they are strayed from me, I know not how."

<small>Beauty in the Visible</small> "But I saw not yet, whereon this weighty matter turned in Thy wisdom, O Thou Omnipotent, *who only doest wonders;* and my mind ranged through corporeal forms; and 'fair,' I defined and distinguished what is so in itself, and 'fit,' whose beauty is in correspondence to some other thing: and this I supported by corporeal examples. And I turned to the nature of the mind; but the false notion which I had of spiritual things let me not see the truth. Yet the force of truth did of itself flash into mine eyes, and I turned away my panting soul from incorporeal substance to lineaments, and colours, and bulky magnitudes. And not being able to see these in the mind, I thought I could not see my mind. And whereas in virtue I loved peace, and in viciousness I abhorred discord; in the first I observed an unity, but in the other a sort of division. And in

that unity, I conceived the rational soul, and the nature of truth and of the chief good to consist: but in this division I miserably imagined there to be some unknown substance of irrational life, and the nature of the chief evil, which should not only be a substance, but real life also, and yet not derived from Thee, O my God, of whom are all things. And yet that first I called a Monad, as it had been a soul without sex; but the latter a Duad; anger, in deeds of violence, and in flagitiousness, lust; not knowing whereof I spake. For I had not known or learned, that neither was evil a substance, nor our soul that chief and unchangeable good."

23. The following passage shows how little the Aristotelian Logic was able to satisfy the cravings of the young student for absolute Goodness and Truth :—

"What did it profit me, that scarce twenty years old, a book of Aristotle, which they call the ten Predicaments, falling into my hands (on whose very name I hung, as on something great and divine, so often as my rhetoric master of Carthage, and others, accounted learned, mouthed it with cheeks bursting with pride,) I read and understood it unaided? On my conferring with others, who said that they scarcely understood it with very able tutors, not only orally explaining it, but drawing many things in sand, they could tell me no more of it than I had learned, reading it by myself. And the book appeared to me to speak very clearly of substances, such as 'man,' and of their qualities, as the figure of a man, of what sort it is; and stature, how many feet high; and his relationship, whose brother he is; or where placed; or when born; or whether he stands or sits; or be shod or armed; or does, or suffers any thing; and all the innumerable things which might be ranged under these nine Predicaments, of which I have given some specimens, or under that chief Predicament of Substance.' <sidenote>The Predicaments.</sidenote>

"What did all this further me, seeing it even hindered me? when, imagining whatever was, was comprehended under those ten Predicaments, I essayed in such wise to understand, O my God, Thy wonderful and unchangeable Unity also, as if Thou also hadst been subjected to Thine own greatness or beauty; so that (as in bodies) they should exist in Thee, as their subject: whereas Thou Thyself art Thy greatness and beauty; but a body is not great or fair in that it is a body, seeing that, though it were less great or fair, it should notwithstanding be a body." <sidenote>Beauty and Unity not conditions of God's Nature, but the very Nature.</sidenote>

24. His addiction to the Manicheans, his longing for Faustus, the promise of unbounded illumination from him on questions which the other members of the sect had not been able to resolve, and his grievous disappointment, are memorable and

well-known facts in his history. The following extract from the 5th Book explains the relation of his theory of Evil to the Christian Theology which he had partly received from his mother.

<small>Evil supposed to have bulk.</small>
"For hence I believed Evil also to be some such kind of substance, and to have its own foul, and hideous bulk; whether gross, which they called earth, or thin and subtile, (like the body of the air,) which they imagine to be some malignant mind, creeping through that earth. And because a piety, such as it was, constrained me to believe, that the good God never created any evil nature, I conceived two masses, contrary to one another, both unbounded, but the evil narrower, the good more expansive. And from this pestilent beginning, the other sacrilegious conceits followed on me. For when my mind endeavoured to recur to the Catholic faith, I was driven back, since that was not the Catholic faith, which I thought to be so. And I seemed to myself more reverential, if I believed of Thee, my God, (to whom Thy mercies confess out of my mouth,) as unbounded, at least on other sides, although on that one where the mass of evil was opposed to Thee, I was constrained to confess Thee bounded; than if on all sides I should imagine Thee to be bounded by the form of a human body. And it seemed to me better to believe Thee to have created no evil, (which to me ignorant seemed not some only, but a bodily substance, because I could not conceive of mind, unless as a subtile body, and that diffused in definite spaces,) than to believe the nature of evil, such as I conceived it, could come from Thee. Yea, and our Saviour himself, Thy Only Begotten, I believed to have been reached forth (as it were) for our salvation, out of the mass of Thy most lucid substance, so as to believe nothing of Him, but what I could imagine in my vanity. His nature, then, being such, I thought could not be born of the Virgin Mary, without being mingled with the flesh: and how that which I had so figured to myself, could be mingled, and not defiled, I saw not."

25. His Pantheistical stage of mind is strikingly described in the 7th book:—

<small>The Corruptible and Incorruptible.</small>
"I, a man, and such a man, sought to conceive of Thee the sovereign, only, true God; and I did in my inmost soul believe that thou wert incorruptible, and uninjurable, and unchangeable; because though not knowing whence or how, yet I saw plainly and was sure, that that which may be corrupted, must be inferior to that which cannot; what could not be injured I preferred unhesitatingly to what could receive injury; the unchangeable to things subject to change. My heart passionately cried out against all my phantoms, and with this one blow I sought to beat away from the eye of my mind all

that unclean troop which buzzed around it. And lo, being scarce put off, in the twinkling of an eye they gathered again thick about me, flew against my face, and beclouded it; so that though not under the form of the human body, yet was I constrained to conceive of Thee (that incorruptible, uninjurable, and unchangeable, which I preferred before the corruptible, and injurable, and changeable) as being in space, whether infused into the world, or diffused infinitely without it. Because whatsoever I conceived, deprived of this space, seemed to me nothing, yea altogether nothing, not even a void, as if a body were taken out of its place, and the place should remain empty of any body at all, of earth and water, air and heaven, yet would it remain a void place, as it were a spacious nothing.

"I then being thus gross-hearted, nor clear even to myself, whatsoever was not extended over certain spaces, nor diffused, nor condensed, nor swelled out, or did not or could not receive some of these dimensions, I thought to be altogether nothing. For over such forms as my eyes are wont to range, did my heart then range: nor yet did I see that this same notion of the mind, whereby I formed those very images, was not of this sort, and yet it could not have formed them, had not itself been some great thing. So also did I endeavour to conceive of Thee, Life of my life, as vast, through infinite spaces, on every side penetrating the whole mass of the universe, and beyond it, every way, through unmeasurable boundless spaces; so that the earth should have Thee, the heaven have Thee, all things have Thee, and they be bounded in Thee, and Thou bounded no where. For that as the body of this air which is above the earth, hindereth not the light of the sun from passing through it, penetrating it, not by bursting or by cutting, but by filling it wholly: so I thought the body not of heaven, air, and sea only, but of the earth too, pervious to Thee, so that in all its parts, the greatest as the smallest, it should admit Thy presence, by a secret inspiration, within and without, directing all things which Thou hast created. So I guessed, only as unable to conceive aught else, for it was false. For thus should a greater part of the earth contain a greater portion of Thee, and a less, a lesser: and all things should in such sort be full of Thee, that the body of an elephant should contain more of Thee than that of a sparrow, by how much larger it is, and takes up more room; and thus shouldest Thou make the several portions of Thyself present unto the several portions of the world, in fragments, large to the large, petty to the petty. But such art not Thou."

<small>Struggles to bring God under the limits of Space.</small>

26. The question of Evil was still the all-absorbing one, whatever others might grow out of it. The following extract shews how he began to connect it with himself:—

"Whatever it were, I perceived it was in such wise to be sought out, as should not constrain me to believe the immutable God to be mutable, lest I should become that evil I was seeking out. I sought it out then, thus far free from anxiety, certain of the untruth of what the Manichees held, from whom I shrunk with my whole heart: for I saw, that through enquiring the origin of evil, they were filled with evil, in that they preferred to think that Thy substance did suffer ill than their own did commit it.

Certainty of a Will.

"And I strained to perceive what I now heard, that freewill was the cause of our doing ill, and Thy just judgment, of our suffering ill. But I was not able clearly to discern it. So then endeavouring to draw my soul's vision out of that deep pit, I was again plunged therein, and endeavouring often I was plunged back as often. But this raised me a little into Thy light, that I knew as well that I had a will, as that I lived: when then I did will or nill any thing, I was most sure, that no other than myself did will and nill: and I all but saw that there was the cause of my sin. But what I did against my will, I saw that I suffered rather than did, and I judged not to be my fault, but my punishment; whereby, however, holding thee to be just, I speedily confessed myself to be not unjustly punished, But again I said, Who made me? Did not my God, who is not only good, but goodness itself? Whence then came I to will evil and nill good, so that I am thus justly punished? who set this in me, and ingrafted into me this plant of bitterness, seeing I was wholly formed by my most sweet God? If the devil were the author, whence is that same devil? And if he also by his own perverse will, of a good angel became a devil, whence, again, came in him that evil will, whereby he became a devil, seeing the whole nature of angels was made by that most good Creator? By these thoughts I was again sunk down and choked; yet not brought down to that hell of error, (where no man confesseth unto Thee,) to think rather that Thou dost suffer ill, than that man doth it.

The world without and within.

27. This discovery that Evil was close to the seeker of it, and that he was projecting it from himself into the circumstances in which he was placed, and into the nature of the Being who had ordained them, is brought out more fully afterwards.

"I sought, 'whence is evil,' and sought in an evil way; and saw not the evil in my very search. I set now before the sight of my spirit, the whole creation, whatsoever we can see therein, (as sea, earth, air, stars, trees, mortal creatures;) yea, and whatever in it we do not see, as the firmament of heaven, all angels, moreover, and all the spiritual inhabitants thereof. But these very beings, as though they were bodies,

WHAT HAS DISTURBED THE UNIVERSE?

did my fancy dispose in place, and I made one great mass of Thy creation, distinguished as to the kinds of bodies; some, real bodies, some, what myself had feigned for spirits. And this mass I made huge, not as it was, (which I could not know,) but as I thought convenient, yet every way finite. But Thee, O Lord, I imagined on every part environing and penetrating it, though every way infinite: as if there were a sea, every where, and on every side, through unmeasured space, one only boundless sea, and it contained within it some sponge, huge, but bounded; that sponge must needs, in all its parts, be filled from that unmeasureable sea; so conceived I Thy creation, itself finite, full of Thee, the Infinite, and I said, Behold God, and behold what God hath created: and God is good, yea, most mightily and incomparably better than all these: but yet He, the Good, created them good; and see how He environeth them, and ful-fills them. Where is evil then, and whence, and how crept it in hither? What is its root, and what its seed? Or hath it no being? Why then fear we and avoid what is not? Or if we fear it idly, then is that very fear evil, whereby the soul is thus idly goaded and racked. Yea, and so much a greater evil, as we have nothing to fear, and yet do fear. Therefore either is that evil which we fear, or else evil is, that we fear. Whence is it then? seeing God, the Good, hath created all these things good. He indeed, the greater and chiefest Good, hath created these lesser goods; still both Creator and created, all are good. Whence is evil? Or, was there some evil matter of which He made, and formed, and ordered it, yet left something in it, which He did not convert into good? Why so then? Had He no might to turn and change the whole, so that no evil should remain in it, seeing He is All-mighty? Lastly, why would He make any thing at all of it, and not rather by the same Allmightiness cause it not to be at all? Or, could it then be, against his will? Or if it were from eternity, why suffered He it so to be for infinite spaces of time past, and was pleased so long after to make something out of it? Or if He were suddenly pleased now to effect somewhat, this rather should the Allmighty have effected, that this evil matter should not be, and He alone be, the whole, true, sovereign, and infinite Good. Or if it was not good that He who was good, should not also frame and create something that were good, then, that evil matter being taken away and brought to nothing, He might form good matter, whereof to create all things. For He should not be Allmighty, if He might not create something good without the aid of that matter which Himself had not created. These thoughts I revolved in my miserable heart, overcharged with most gnawing cares, lest I should die ere I had found the truth;

Good infinite—Whence, then, is Ill?

Dreams of Omnipotence.

yet was the faith of Thy Christ our Lord and Saviour, professed in the Church Catholic, firmly fixed in my heart, in many points, indeed, as yet unformed, and fluctuating from the rule of doctrine; yet did not my mind utterly leave it, but rather daily took in more and more of it."

28. The result of his struggles, after the scripture revelation had become intelligible to him, is contained in the following extract:—

Augustin coming to quietness.

"And being thence admonished to return to myself, I entered even into my inward self, Thou being my Guide: and able I was, for thou wert become my Helper. And I entered and beheld with the eye of my soul, (such as it was,) above the same eye of my soul, above my mind, the Light Unchangeable. Not this ordinary light, which all flesh may look upon, nor as it were a greater of the same kind, as though the brightness of this should be manifold brighter, and with its greatness take up all space. Not such was this light, but other, yea, far other from all these. Nor was it above my soul, as oil is above water, nor yet as heaven above earth: but above to my soul because It made me; and I below It because I was made by It. He that knows the Truth, knows what that Light is; and he that knows It, knows eternity. Love knoweth it. O Truth who art Eternity! and Love Who art Truth! and Eternity who art Love! Thou art my God, to Thee do I sigh night and day. Thee when I first knew thou liftedst me up, that I might see there was

Fear and Wonder.

what I might see, and that I was not yet such as to see. And Thou didst beat back the weakness of my sight, streaming forth thy beams of light upon me most strongly, and I trembled with love and awe: and I perceived myself to be far off from Thee, in the region of unlikeness, as if I heard this Thy voice from on high: 'I am the food of grown men; grow, and thou shalt feed upon Me; nor shalt thou convert Me, like the food of thy flesh, into thee, but thou shalt be converted into Me.' And I learned, that *Thou for iniquity chastenest man, and Thou madest my soul to consume away like a spider.* And I said, 'Is Truth therefore nothing, because it is not diffused through space finite or infinite?' And thou criedst to me from afar; 'Yea verily, *I AM that I AM.*' And I heard, as the heart heareth, nor had I room to doubt, and I should sooner doubt that I live, than that truth is not, *which is clearly seen being understood by those things which are made.*

That which is and is not.

"And I beheld the other things below Thee, and I perceived, that they neither altogether are, nor altogether are not, for they are, since they are from Thee, but are not, because they are not, what Thou art. For that truly is, which remains unchangeably. *It is good then for me to hold fast unto God;* for if I remain not in Him, I cannot in myself; but *He remaining in himself reneweth all things. And thou art the Lord my God, since Thou standest not in need of my goodness.*

"And it was manifested unto me, that those things be good, which yet are corrupted; which neither were they sovereignly good, nor unless they were good, could be corrupted: for if sovereignly good they were incorruptible, if not good at all, there were nothing in them to be corrupted. For corruption injures, but unless it diminished goodness, it could not injure. Either then corruption injures not, which cannot be; or which is most certain, all which is corrupted is deprived of good. But if they be deprived of all good, they shall cease to be. For if they shall be, and can now no longer be corrupted, they shall be better than before, because they shall abide incorruptibly. And what more monstrous than to affirm things to become better by losing all their good? Therefore, if they shall be deprived of all good, they shall no longer be. So long therefore as they are, they are good: therefore whatsoever is, is good. That evil then which I sought, whence it is, is not any substance: for were it a substance, it should be good. For either it should be an incorruptible substance, and so a chief good: or a corruptible substance; which unless it were good, could not be corrupted. I perceived therefore, and it was manifested to me, that Thou madest all things good, nor is there any substance at all, which Thou madest not; and for that Thou madest not all things equal, therefore are all things; because each is good, and altogether very good, because our God *made all things very good.*

The loss of Good.

"And to Thee is nothing whatsoever evil: yea, not only to Thee, but also to Thy creation as a whole, because there is nothing without, which may break in, and corrupt that order which Thou hast appointed it. But in the parts thereof, some things, because unharmonizing with other some, are accounted evil: whereas those very things harmonise with others, and are good; and in themselves are good. And all these things which harmonise not together, do yet with the inferior part, which we call Earth, having its own cloudy and windy sky harmonising with it. Far be it then that I should say, 'These things should not be:' for should I see nought but these, I should indeed long for the better; but still must even for these alone praise Thee; for that Thou art to be *praised,* do shew *from the earth, dragons and all deeps, fire, hail, snow, ice, and stormy wind, which fulfil Thy word; mountains, and all hills, fruitful trees, and all cedars; beasts, and all cattle, creeping things, and flying fowls'; kings of the earth, and all people, princes, and all judges of the earth; young men and maidens, old men and young, praise Thy Name.* But when, from heaven, these *praise Thee, praise Thee,*

Good in God.

our God, in the heights, all Thy angels, all Thy hosts, sun and moon, all the stars and light, the Heaven of heavens, and the waters that be above the heavens, praise Thy Name;* I did not now long for things better, because I conceived of all: and with a sounder judgment I apprehended that the things above were better than these below, but all together better than those above by themselves.

All things good.
"There is no soundness in them, whom aught of Thy creation displeaseth: as neither in me, when much that Thou hast made displeased me. And because my soul durst not be displeased at my God, it would fain not account that Thine which displeased it. Hence it had gone into the opinion of two substances, and had no rest, but talked idly. And returning thence, it had made to itself a God, through infinite measures of all space, and thought it to be Thee, and placed it in its heart, and had again become the temple of its own idol, to Thee abominable. But after Thou hadst soothed my head, unknown to me, and closed *mine eyes that they should not behold vanity*, I ceased somewhat of my former self, and my frenzy was lulled to sleep; and I awoke in Thee, and saw thee infinite, but in another way, and this sight was not derived from the flesh.

Evil no Substance.
"And I looked back on other things, and I saw that they owed their being to Thee, and were all bounded in Thee, but in a different way; not as being in space, but because Thou containest all things in Thine hand in Thy Truth; and all things are true so far as they be; nor is there any falsehood, unless when that is thought to be which is not. And I saw that all things did harmonize, not with their places only, but with their seasons; and that Thou, who only art Eternal, didst not begin to work after innumerable spaces of times spent; for that all spaces of times, both which have passed, and which shall pass, neither go nor come but through Thee, working and abiding.

"And I perceived and found it nothing strange, that bread which is pleasant to a healthy palate is loathsome to one distempered; and to sore eyes light is offensive, which to the sound is delightful. And thy righteousness displeaseth the wicked; much more the viper and reptiles, which Thou hast created good, fitting in with the inferior portions of Thy Creation, with which the very wicked also fit in; and that the more, by how much they be unlike Thee; but with the superior creatures, by how much they become more like to Thee. And I inquired what iniquity was, and found it to be no substance, but the perversion of the will, turned aside from Thee, O God, the Supreme, towards these lower things, and *casting out its bowels*, and puffed up outwardly.

"And I wondered that I now loved Thee, and no phantasm

for Thee. And yet did I not press on to enjoy my God, but was borne up to Thee by Thy beauty, and soon borne down from Thee by mine own weight, sinking with sorrow into these inferior things. This weight was carnal custom. Yet dwelt there with me a remembrance of Thee; nor did I any way doubt that there was One to whom I might cleave, but that I was not yet such as to cleave to Thee; for that *the body which is corrupted presseth down the soul, and the earthly tabernacle weigheth down the mind that museth upon many things.* And most certain I was *that Thy invisible works from the creation of the world are clearly seen, being understood by the things that are made, even Thy eternal power and Godhead.* For examining whence it was that I admired the beauty of bodies celestial or terrestrial, and what aided me in judging soundly on things mutable, and pronouncing, 'This ought to be thus, this not:' examining, I say, whence it was that I so judged, seeing I did so judge, I had found the unchangeable and true Eternity of Truth, above my changeable mind. And thus, by degrees, I passed from bodies to the soul, which through the bodily senses perceives; and thence to its inward faculty, to which the bodily senses represent things external, whitherto reaches the faculties of beasts: and thence again to the reasoning faculty, to which what is received from the senses of the body is referred to be judged. Which finding itself also to be in me a thing variable, raised itself up to its own understanding, and drew away my thoughts from the power of habit, withdrawing itself from those troops of contradictory phantasms; that so it might find what that light was whereby it was bedewed when, without all doubting, it cried out, 'That the unchangeable was to be preferred to the changeable'; whence also it knew That Unchangeable, which, unless it had in some way known, it had had no sure ground to prefer it to the changeable. And thus with the flash of one trembling glance it arrived at THAT WHICH IS; and then I saw Thy *invisible things understood by the things which are made.* But I could not fix my gaze thereon; and my infirmity being struck back, I was thrown again on my wonted habits, carrying along with me only a loving memory thereof, and a longing for what I had, as it were, perceived the odour of, but was not yet able to feed on."

Love of God.

The τὸ ὄν. He who is.

29. These passages concern the growth of his belief. There are others of very great significance, which embody some of his later discoveries. Strictly speaking, they should be postponed to those philosophical treatises of which we propose to speak presently; but as they occur in the "Confessions," we cannot be blamed for inserting them here. The following on Eternity and Time is particularly profound and suggestive:—

Eternity and Time.

"Who speak thus, do not yet understand Thee, O Wisdom of God, Light of souls,—understand not yet how the things be made, which by Thee and in Thee are made: yet they strive to comprehend things eternal, whilst their heart fluttereth between the motions of things past and to come, and is still unstable. Who shall hold it, and fix it, that it be settled awhile, and awhile catch the glory of that ever-fixed Eternity, and compare it with the times which are never fixed, and see that it cannot be compared; and that a long time cannot become long, but out of many motions passing by, which cannot be prolonged altogether; but that in the Eternal nothing passeth, but the whole is present; whereas no time is all at once present: and that all time past is driven on by time to come, and all to come followeth upon the past; and all past and to come is created, and flows out of that which is ever present? Who shall hold the heart of man, that it may stand still, and see how eternity ever stillstanding, neither past nor to come, uttereth the times past and to come? Can my hand do this, or the hand of my mouth by speech bring about a thing so great?"

Yesterday and to-day.

"Nor dost Thou by time precede time: else shouldest Thou not precede all times. But Thou precedest all things past, by the sublimity of an ever-present eternity; and surpassest all future because they are future, and when they come they shall be past; *but Thou art the Same, and thy years fail not.* Thy years neither come nor go; whereas ours both come and go, that they all may come. Thy years stand together, because they do stand; nor are departing thrust out by coming years, for they pass not away; but ours shall all be, when they shall no more be. Thy years are one day; and Thy day is not daily, but To-day, seeing Thy To-day gives not place unto to-morrow, for neither doth it replace yesterday. Thy To-day is Eternity; therefore didst Thou beget The Coeternal, to whom Thou saidst, *This day have I begotten Thee.* Thou hast made all things; and before all times Thou art; neither in any time was time not.

"At no time then hadst Thou not made any thing, because time itself Thou madest. And no times are coeternal with Thee, because Thou abidest; but if they abode, they should not be times. For what is time? Who can readily and briefly explain this? Who can even in thought comprehend it, so as to utter a word about it? But what in discourse do we mention more familiarly and knowingly, than time? And, we understand, when we speak of it; we understand also, when we hear it spoken of by another. What then is time? If no one asks me, I know: if I wish to explain it to one that asketh, I know not: yet I say boldly, that I know, that if nothing passed away, time past were not; and if nothing were coming, a time to come were not; and if nothing were, time present were not. Those two times then, past and to come, how are they, seeing the past now is not, and that to come is not yet? But the present, should it always be present, and never pass into time past, verily it should not be time, but eternity. If time present (if it is to be time) only cometh into existence, because it passeth into time past, how can we say that either this is, whose cause of being is, that it shall not be; so, namely, that we cannot truly say that time is, but because it is tending not to be? [sidenote: For ever.]

"And yet we say, 'a long time' and 'a short time;' still, only of time past or to come. A long time past (for example) we call an hundred years since; and a long time to come, an hundred years hence. But a short time past, we call (suppose) ten days since; and a short time to come, ten days hence. But in what sense is that long or short, which is not? For the past, is not now; and the future, is not yet. Let us not then say, 'it is long;' but of the past, 'it hath been long;' and of the future, 'it will be long.' O my Lord, my Light, shall not here also Thy Truth mock at man? For that past time which was long, was it long when it was now past, or when it was yet present? For then might it be long, when there was, what could be long; but when past, it was no longer; wherefore neither could that be long, which was not at all. Let us not then say, 'time past hath been long:' for we shall not find, what hath been long, seeing that since it was past, it is no more; but let us say, 'that present time was long;' because, when it was present, it was long. For it had not yet passed away, so as not to be; and therefore there was, what could be long; but after it was past, that ceased also to be long, which ceased to be." [sidenote: Past and Present.]

"What now is clear and plain is, that neither things to come nor past are. Nor is it properly said, 'there be three times, past, present, and to come:' yet perchance it might be properly said, 'there be three times; a present of things past, a present of things present, and a present of things future.' For these three do exist in some sort, in the soul, but otherwhere do I not see them; present of things past, memory; present of things present, sight; present of things future, expectation. If thus we be permitted to speak, I see three times, and I confess there are three. Let it be said too, 'there be three times, past, present, and to come:' in our incorrect way. See, I object not, nor gainsay, nor find fault, if what is so said be but understood, that neither what is to be, now is, nor what is past. For but few things are there, which we speak properly, most things improperly; still the things intended are understood."*

* The extracts from the " Confessions" have been taken from the translation in the Oxford Library of the Fathers.

110 CHRISTIAN PHILOSOPHY.

The book Contra Academicos.

30. Shortly before his baptism Augustin wrote three books "*Against the Academics.*" They give us a very delightful picture of his inner mind and of his social life at this crisis of his history. His new discoveries have not carried him into violent hostility with the thoughts or the friends of earlier days :—they have given him a deeper and livelier interest in both. Augustin is still the Philosopher; nay, is urging all over whom he has influence to become philosophers. He speaks of the pursuit of Wisdom as that into which he has been gradually led out of a mere windy profession by grief of heart; and he addresses his books to Romanianus,—a man, it would appear, of highly cultivated tastes, who had plunged into the luxury of the capital, who had been the most sumptuous and popular of citizens, but who, "as he cared to be liberal rather than rich, as he never desired to be more powerful than just," has been brought under the discipline of suffering that he might be led into a love of the true, and not merely of the beautiful. Augustin speaks of this treatise in the "Retractations" as written "when he had betaken himself to the rest of the Christian life." It was natural that in looking back upon it after many years, and in very changed circumstances, he should find something to complain of in it, and that he should not be able quite to reproduce his then state of feeling. But his self-accusations are not serious, and need not expose him to any very severe judgments from us. He thinks that he used the word "fortune" too carelessly, and too like a heathen, though he hinted that it was only a name for some secret order of providence : he speaks of a fable, in the second book, from which we must confess that we have received much profit and encouragement, concerning the two sisters, Philocalia and Philosophia, as silly and impertinent : and, as might perhaps be expected and feared, he thinks his language respecting the Academics was too courteous, and the reverence he expresses for Plato a little dangerous. As there are no other censures, we may presume that he considered the substance of the dialogues sound and profitable.

c. 3. Mundi hujus dona quæ meipsum capere moliebantur quotidie ista cantantem nisi me pectoris dolor ventosam professionem abjicere et in philosophiæ gremium confugere coegisset.

Retract. lib. i. c. 1: Cùm ergo religuissem vel quæ adeptus fueram in cupiditatibus hujus mundi vel quæ adipisci volebam et me ad Christianæ vitæ otium contulissem nondum baptizatus, etc.

Id. cc. 2, 3.

C. 3: Prorsùs inepta estet insulsa illa fabula de Philocalia et Philosophia.

Object of these Dialogues.

31. Their main object, as we might infer from the persons against whom they are directed, is to show that investigation, however interesting and worthy of all zeal when there is something to be investigated, cannot be an ultimate object,—that uncertainty and a perpetual equilibrium of mind are not desirable,—that Truth is to be sought because it can be found. Here, no doubt, is the link between Augustin's Philosophy and his Divinity; between his energy in study and his confidence of a revelation from above. The Academical theory, or rather the Academical tendency, had been to himself, and was, he saw, to a number, the greatest hindrance to practical belief, precisely because it was the hindrance to manly and hopeful in-

quiry. Acquiescence in doubt is only another name for acquiescence in sensual gratifications. If the mind has nothing actual to grasp, the body which has, must maintain its superiority: the repose of the Epicurean dogmatist lies very near to the restlessness of the pseudo-Platonical sceptic. Augustin, therefore, might well feel that this was to be his first battle; that unless he could shake the doctrine which affirms that nothing can be known, a Gospel professing to enunciate the highest knowledge would be always pronounced impossible.

32. But the method which he adopts for this purpose is as unlike that of a dogmatist of the Tertullian school as can well be conceived. Licentius, the son of Romanianus, and Trygetius, are pupils of Augustin. The former he holds up to the example of his father, as an earnest and devoted student; the latter had for a time betaken himself to the army, but had returned with fresh zest to the kind of warfare into which Augustin was so well able to initiate him. The Christian neophyte, it might be supposed, would rather deter these youths from debates and arguments, and treat them as only fit to receive what he gave them. On the contrary, he himself puts them upon a trial of strength, urging them to canvass the whole question which was at issue between the Academicians and their opponents. The boys enter the lists with hearty good-will, their master from time to time interfering, not to check their ardour but to encourage it, to help either party in recovering any ground which he had unwittingly lost, to hinder them from taking any unfair advantages, to show them the duty of making sacrifices of favourable positions for the sake of attaining the ultimate end, which is not victory but truth. As a specimen of a kind, and a very valuable kind, of practical education, the book may take its place by Milton's Letter to Mr. Hartlib, or the treatises of Mr. and Miss Edgeworth. But it is also exceedingly instructive as showing that the Academicians could be most effectively answered by one who understood their method best. Long before the final result is attained, we feel that the young men are in training to be believers in Truth, that they have learnt how well that is worth fighting for, and that nothing else is worth fighting for.

Augustin as a school master.

Contra Academicos, lib. i. c. 4.

Id. c. 4.

33. Throughout this lively and interesting discussion the question is always recurring, whether a blessed life can be separated from the knowledge of Truth. It was the characteristic doctrine of Augustin that one was involved in the other,—that the knowledge of truth, however obtained, did not procure blessedness, but was blessedness,—that without it man is miserable. There is a special book on the blessed life. It was written at the same time with those on the Academics. The

The book De Beatâ Vitâ.

occasion of it is stated thus in his dedication to Theodorus:—
"In the ides of November was my birthday. There were present, first, my mother Monnica, my brother Navigius, Trygetius and Licentius my fellow-citizens and disciples, and I would not have my cousins Lastidianus and Rusticus away, for though they cannot endure the schools, I thought their common sense would be of great help in the subject I proposed to discuss. Lastly, there was one among us, the youngest of all, but with a disposition which promises, if love does not deceive me, something very great,—my son Adeodatus." The discussion which takes place after a light repast opens with the question, "whether the soul does not require food as well as the body?" Thence comes the inquiry, "what the appetite of the soul is—what is its satisfaction?" The appetite is shown to be, for the Infinite and Eternal. He is blessed then who has God. But of whom can that be affirmed? Licentius answered, "He possesses God who lives well." Trygetius answered, "He possesses God who does what God wills to be done." The boy said, "He possesses God who hath a pure heart." Monnica approved all the sentiments,—this last most. Navigius and Rusticus were silent! These solemn and reverent utterances do not prevent Augustin from introducing again some of those philosophical topics which occupied us in the former dialogues. The discourse, with all its depth and earnestness, is often pleasant, even humorous. There is evidently a sense in the mind of all the guests at Augustin's feast, that the blessedness which they seek for is within the reach of all, and that each is helping the other to attain it and enjoy it. A divine conversation has seldom been carried on with more of human friendliness and grace, or with a more evident feeling that all outward and sensible beauties ought to be relished and enjoyed by him who has the highest and the most inward.

34. We can but allude to two books on Order which follow these. Why Augustin should have entered upon such a subject will be sufficiently intelligible to those who have traced the growth of his mind in the "Confessions." He found one of two perils threatening him: either God's Providence did not descend into the deepest and minutest things; or else, evil was to be ascribed to Him. Augustin bravely declares, that though the first error is a very great one, the other is much more terrible. It is better to charge Him with negligence than with malice and cruelty. The question, then, as he expresses it in his "Retractations," "whether the Order of Divine Providence containeth all things good as well as evil," is one which the author of the book on the Blessed Life was almost obliged to set before himself and his disciples. But he adds, "When I

saw that this matter, difficult to be understood in itself, could scarcely be brought at all to the perception of those with whom I had to do, by any process of disputation, I preferred to speak about the order of study whereby we may advance from corporeal to incorporeal things." This explanation will account for some disappointment which the reader may experience when the author digresses into stories respecting Licentius and Monnica, and passes from high considerations of Divine Providence into questions about grammar, music, poetry, dialectic, rhetoric, geometry, astronomy,—valuable and important in themselves, but not exactly what the title of the book had led us to expect. C. 22, &c.
Lib. ii. c. 12, 13, and 14.

29. The two books of Soliloquies exhibit the deep conviction in Augustin's mind, that the eternal life of man's spirit and the knowledge of truth are inseparable. The passages at the close of the second book, concerning the Memory, lead us into the very heart of Platonical doctrine. We should be inclined to doubt whether any Latin, before or since, ever entered into it so deeply. The treatise, both for its method and its results, is worthy of the most serious meditation of any student, as a commentary upon the ancient wisdom, and as an induction to that of the Middle Ages. The book on the Immortality of the Soul, Augustin says in his "Retractations," is so obscure, from the contortion of the thoughts and its brevity, that he could scarcely understand it himself. The account in the same honest record, of the book De Quantitate Animæ, will best explain its object: "In the same city I wrote a dialogue in which there are many questions and discussions concerning the soul: whence it is, of what nature, what its greatness, why it was assigned to a body, what effect is produced upon it by its conjunction with a body—what effect by its departure from the body. But seeing that the question—how great it is—is discussed there with much diligence and subtlety that I might show its magnitude not to be a corporeal magnitude, and yet that it has a magnitude of its own, therefore from this single inquiry the whole has taken its name." A criticism upon a passage in this treatise, "that the soul seems to have brought all arts with it, and that learning is nothing else than recollection," shows that the old Bishop had not abandoned all the thoughts of the young student, though he feared to indorse them and to sanction all the inferences which might be drawn from them. The great question of the treatise—how to connect the thoughts of length, of breadth, of height, all that we attribute to mathematical figures, with spiritual substances—is one which has occupied serious men at all times, and which does not cease to occupy us when we forget it. Few doubt The books of Soliloquies.

Cap. 20, § 34 and 35.

De Immortalitate Animæ, Retract. lib. i. cap. 5.

The book De Quantitate Animæ, Retract. lib. i. cap. 8.

that language expresses a connection between the two worlds: *what* it indicates respecting the nature of the connection is the difficulty which all in some way or other have been trying to solve. If Augustin does not solve it, he at least makes us feel how it arises, how it is involved in all our common speech, how it may beset those who take most pains to give an account of their thoughts and their words. When we say that Augustin discusses the relation between Reason and Ratiocination, and between Sense and Science,—that he inquires how far science and reason exist in beasts,—whether the soul knows of itself,— whether it is said to grow really or metaphorically,—we have indicated how near he has touched many of the controversies of the most modern world. And his description of the seven degrees of the soul's ascent is a preparation for some of the most curious parts of the practical divinity as well as of the moral philosophy of the later Church.

C. 27 and 29.

C. 20 and 21.

The books on Music.
30. Long as have been our commentaries on Augustin, we cannot quite resolve to pass unmentioned the six books on Music, because it is evident that the thoughts which are expressed in them soothed the mind of the writer after the conflicts of his earlier years, and because he looked back upon them with great tenderness in his mature life. These six books, he says, are on Rhythm; he should have added six more on Melody, if the burden of his ecclesiastical duties had not made all such delights impossible. He is sure there is a passage by regular stages from these corporeal and changeable numbers, to the unchangeable which are in the immutable Truth itself; that through them we may strive after those inmost mysteries where Wisdom joyfully meets those who love her."

The Master. Nor can we forget the little book on "the Master," which is so much the more interesting and striking, because it is a conversation with the child who reminded him of his youthful errors, and for whom he so frankly and courageously at all times expresses his affection; and because it exhibits the method of his own teaching as well as his idea of the highest teacher. These

Later Treatises.
are his properly philosophical books. Those "On Free-will," "On the Manners of the Church, and the Manicheans," and the more elaborate and better-known treatise "On the City of God," though strictly theological, are full of passages which throw light upon his philosophy, and ought to be considered by all who wish thoroughly to understand it.

CHAPTER V.

THE FIFTH CENTURY.

1. A CENTURY which opens with the reigns of Arcadius and Honorius holds out small promise of blessings to mankind in the east or in the west. Yet it is one rich in the materials of history, if not in history itself, one which no philosopher can pass over, whatever he may think of its contributions to philosophy. The theological battles of the Greek church and the Greek empire, which aroused the most violent and the pettiest passions of Egyptians, Syrians, and Byzantines, pointed to principles in which all ages and countries are alike interested. Nestorius and Eutyches may be treated by many merely as movers of subtleties which have no significance for the world; the councils which strove to silence them, merely as haughty and ferocious dogmatists. There is excuse enough for each charge. But the question, whether there is a divine foundation for man's life, and whether that is also a human foundation, was involved in these controversies; the philosophers who most hated and despised the Church were really engaged in them as much as its members could be. We cannot interpret Proclus any more than Cyril, if we overlook them, or do not remember what multitudes of hearts were occupied with them. How such debates should have anything to do with the stirring events which were changing the condition of society in western Europe, with the sacking of Rome, the occupation of the different provinces by Visigoths or Vandals, the overthrow of the Western Empire, the establishment of Paganism in Britain, of Frankish orthodoxy in Gaul, we may find it hard at first to discover. And yet the schools and the world were in this time, as in all times, interpreters of each other. The principles which men were acting out in one sphere were those on which they were tormenting their thoughts in the other. We must understand what concerned the *people* if we would know what is meant by the speculations of those who strove most to keep aloof from them, and affected most to despise them.

Theological disputes of the fifth century.

Philosophers engaged in them really if not directly.

Outward events of the time.

Their relation to philosophy.

2. The struggles between the Neo-Platonic school and the Christian Church belong as much to this century as to the last. But the Church has won an outward triumph. The sages can

116   THE TWO CITIES.

War of the Church with the Neo-Platonists. have little hope of finding another imperial champion. When the temple of Serapis was thrown down by the Christian zealots in Egypt, stirred up by the unprincipled Bishop Theophilus, a sign was given that the rites of Paganism belonged to the past and not to the present. They might be loved all the more by the antiquarian and sentimentalist, but a leader of armies, even if he had all Julian's natural taste and acquired cultivation, could scarcely seek to re-establish them. Hence an evident *Change in the position and character of the combatants.* change is visible on both sides. A predominance of mysticism over every other tendency is characteristic of the Heathen devotee. Practical wisdom, degenerating in most cases into worldly wisdom, becomes characteristic of the Churchman. The one asserts the invisible as his possession, and only now and then dreams that he may master the visible. The other begins to think that that is given to him to use and to rule; the *The Church governing.* spiritual region, the Kingdom of Heaven, he claims as his too, but often chiefly that he may exclude the rest of men from it. The noble-hearted Chrysostom is as essentially a practical and governing man as the proud and unscrupulous Cyril. Even Augustin in this century becomes more occupied with the management of the African Church, and with Donatist quarrels, than with the transcendant thoughts of his earlier years.

Alexandria. 3. We have spoken much of Alexandria in former centuries. This city was still to be the focus of philosophical thought and philosophical contentions. There it was that the Church and the Schools stood out in formal opposition to each other; there both were exhibited in their glory and their humiliation, there the practical power of the Christian faith as a ruler of the world, there the detestable crimes of many of its professors, presented themselves in glaring contrast to the social impotence of the Neo-Platonists, to the high aims of one or two among their *Hypatia.* teachers. The tragedy of Hypatia brings all these aspects of the fifth century together, and prepares us for the downfall of the antichristian sages, for the temporary triumph of something scarcely less antichristian, for the great judgment upon the *Athens.* eastern world, when Alexandria stooped to Mecca. But Athens is the place in which Neo-Platonism flourished comparatively undisturbed by ecclesiastical influences. There philosophy in its nakedness, or as some say in its purity, put forth its last efforts, and endeavoured to crown and unite all the past achievements of Greek schools.

Proclus, A. D. 412-485. 4. A very high authority, M. Cousin, supposes this attempt to have been perfectly successful. The sacred Platonical succession he believes was faithfully and religiously preserved; the torch was transmitted in undimmed lustre from hand to hand; it never burned so brightly as when Proclus resigned it. The following is but a specimen of the language in which he speaks of him. "He was illustrious as a mathematician and an astronomer; he was the first among existing philologers; he had so comprehended all religions in his mind, and paid them such equal reverence, that he was as it were the priest of the whole universe: nor was it wonderful that a man possessing such a high knowledge of nature and science should have this initiation into all sacred mysteries.".........."As he was the head of the Athenian school and of all later philosophy, so I venture to affirm that all the earlier is found gathered up in him, and that he may be taken as the one interpreter of the whole philosophy of the Greeks.".........I shall set it down as an established fact that nothing great was thought out by Iamblichus, Porphyry, and Plotinus, either in ethics, in metaphysics, or in physics, which is not found expressed more clearly and methodically in Proclus.".........."The three-fold division of Greek philosophy may be reduced at last to one, which being the same always, by a natural and certain progress enlarges and unfolds itself, and moves on through three stages intimately connected, the first being contained in the second, the second in the third, so that the man who after the lapse of ages finds himself at the end of this gradually evolving series, on the highest apex of that third age, as he embraces all the accumulations of former times in himself, stands as the representative of each sect of Greece, emphatically *the* Greek philosopher. Such a man I say was Proclus, in whom it seems to me are combined and from whom shine forth in no irregular or uncertain rays all the philosophical lights which have illustrated Greece in various times; to wit Orpheus, Pythagoras, Plato, Aristotle, Zeno, Plotinus, Porphyry, and Iamblichus."

M. Cousin's judgment of him: "Procli Opera, etc., illustravit Victor Cousin: Parisiis, 1820." Præfatio generalis, p. 23. p. 24. P. 25. P. 25 and 26. Unites all Greek wisdom in himself.

5. Besides the weight which this testimony acquires from the learning and genius of M. Cousin, it is more impressive from the country to which he belongs and which he represents. We, and still more our diligent German brethren, are generally supposed to be capable of enduring a considerable amount of tediousness with the tolerance which results from our consciousness of needing the like for our own compositions. But that excellence must be very great indeed which can induce a Frenchman, with his natural liveliness and sense of the ridiculous, to suffer the elaboration through long pages of points which his wit must have reached by a single spring. This, and far more than this, had M. Cousin to bear while he was ascertaining for himself that Proclus was a compendious Orpheus, Pythagoras, Plato, and Aristotle. Thus, for instance, one of the most celebrated of his works is a commentary on the first Alcibiades of Plato. It was evidently a lecture to his class. It aims of course at exhi-

Strangeness of this opinion in a French writer.

Tediousness of Proclus.

biting the particular worth of the dialogue under discussion, but that only for the purpose of elucidating the method and principles of Plato, and of all science. The dialogue opens with these words, "O! son of Cleinias, I think that you sometimes wonder," &c. Considering the great field which the commentator has before him, a dialogue of some compass in itself, and then the gathering together in one the three periods of Greek wisdom, one would have supposed that these words might have been dismissed with some rapidity; that at all events the teacher might have told his pupils at once what Socrates supposed would cause the wonder of Alcibiades. The Athenian youths were in great error if they looked for any such superficial treatment of the subject from Proclus. First of all we have a discussion on the importance of the openings of the dialogues. It must never be supposed that they are mere easy dramatical introductions to what follows. All great principles are involved in them. But, secondly, Socrates says "*I think.*" Why does he say "I think"? Is it not his great object to lead us into science or knowledge, and could he who was guiding other men out of uncertainty and mere opinion be himself subject to such uncertainties? This great difficulty must be cleared up. It must be shewn that there are variable subjects as well as fixed and constant. Aristotle must be quoted to prove that the geometer is not to use rhetoric in his study, nor the rhetorician to apply geometry in persuasion. Necessary things are to be spoken of in necessary language, probable in probable. Moreover, Alcibiades was a hasty and presumptuous youth. It was a peculiarly winning and graceful method of addressing him, to begin with a somewhat doubtful expression of this kind. So that altogether Proclus seems to have proved in the most irrefragable manner, taking the subject out of the region of mere doubt and probability, and bringing it very near to demonstration, that Socrates might consistently with the general maxims and objects of his philosophy use the word " I think" in familiar convesation. But, next, why does he say " Son of Cleinias," when he might have called him simply Alcibiades ? The propriety of this language, too, is established after painful and accurate enquiry. The phrase admits of a partial justification on the grounds that children are advantaged by reflection on the glory of him who begat them, and that Cleinias had distinguished himself in an Athenian war; that Homer is fond of patronymics; that it is an old Greek custom to use them. But there is a far deeper motive: Alcibiades might think of the divine reason from which souls issue, when he was reminded that he was the son of somebody.

6. We do not quote these passages as if they were conclusive

against the opinion of M. Cousin. On the contrary, we believe that opinion to be justified by evidence which must have seemed to the greatest of modern Eclectics quite irresistible. It is not the mistake of a partial admirer that Proclus gathers up the threads of former Greek enquirers, and weaves them into one woof. It is not a mistake that his intense devotion to Plato, to the intermediate commentators upon him, but especially to his own master Syrianus, is often rewarded by apprehensions which justify themselves to every student, and for which we should be very grateful. Nor is there the least doubt that though Proclus talks an infinite deal of nothing, more than any man in Athens, he not unfrequently enunciates a proposition of great worth with a neatness, sharpness, and perspicuity, such as can scarcely be found in the citizen of any city but his. If the conclusion to which we arrive respecting him must be ultimately something very different from that which M. Cousin's eulogium suggests, we are most willing that our readers should know what plea there is for that eulogium, and should admit the claims of Proclus to canonisation in spite of our devil advocacy. Merits of Proclus

7. The lectures on the Alcibiades, of which we have given one or two rather disadvantageous specimens, are not so wholly occupied with transcendental questions that they overlook the characteristics of Alcibiades as a notable historical figure. With some formality and many unnecessary words, but not without real beauty, Proclus developes the character of the love which Socrates bore to him, how different it was from that of all who admired and flattered him, how its whole aim was to draw him away from the restless pursuit of a multitude of objects, and to fix his mind on the real and the abiding. Eight centuries had not passed away without giving even the ordinary commentator certain perceptions on this subject, a certain power of understanding how the higher being stoops from his glory to draw up the inferior after him, how this is effected by sympathy with his weaknesses, by contemplating objects as he contemplates them while yet he retains that elevation of which he wishes his scholar to partake. The ability of describing this as the peculiarity of the best man because it is also the quality of the gods, belongs to the Neo-Platonist more than it did to those at whose feet he sat, and from whom he professed to derive his wisdom. Here especially we discover that change which we have pointed out already as the distinguishing one of the new philosophy, not only that it could not stand apart from theology (for the old Platonism had never tried to do that) but that it assumed theology as its ground and starting-point, not merely as its termination; that it supposed the higher world to have

Idea of Love.

See especially pages 88—109.

Love divine and human.
Ἀτεχνῶς οὖν μοι δοκεῖ Δαίμονος ἀγαθοῦ χώραν ὁ Σωκράτης ἐπέχειν πρὸς τὸν Ἀλκιβιάδην καὶ κατοπτεύειν αὐτὸν ἐκ νεότητος ὥσπερ ἐκεῖνος

καὶ φρουρεῖν καὶ τὰς ἐνεργείας αὐτοῦ πάσας ἐπισκοπεῖν, κ.τ.λ.

Theological character of the love.
[Examine particularly the striking passage, 162, last line, to 173.]

condescended to the lower, not merely the lower to be in a process of ascent towards the higher. We have seen how Plotinus, and still more Porphyry, struggled, the one to restore philosophy to its purer and colder position, the other to preserve it in that position; how inconsistent each was in this experiment, how inevitably the hierophantic doctrines of Iamblichus triumphed over theirs. In the time of Proclus it was no longer a matter of controversy. The war between mythology and philosophy had terminated. Each was acknowledged as necessary to the other. In their battles with the Christian Church, the Neo-Platonists adopted much of its language. Their theory was that its ideas belonged to them, that they were in fact ideas of the old world implied in all that had been written about heroes and philosophers, and the relations between gods and goddesses; that their function was to restore them to their proper owners, at the same time making use of their philosophy to hinder the ideas from being lost in the stories which had embodied them.

The Christian love mixes with the Platonic.

8. Although, therefore, Athens was not the battle-field between Christianity and the new philosophy, and although it would be unjust to impute to Proclus any directly polemical purpose in his commentaries upon Plato, there can be no doubt that he wished his pupils to understand that the Christian idea of love, and all that was connected with it, had already been practically exhibited in the conduct of the earlier philosophers, as well as expressed in the Pagan divinity, and could now be set forth in its most refined and perfect form by those who harmonised them in their all-embracing Eclecticism. It was in this way that Proclus strove to establish his title to be the priest as well as the dialectician of the universe. It was thus that looking back upon all the teachings of the past, and around upon all the faith and superstitions of the present, he sought to extract the essential oil from them, discarding their superfluous materials. The question is, what was the result of the process, how much of this quintessence has he been able to bequeath for the nourishment of mankind? Something unquestionable, as we have said already, we do owe to him. This especially. It might be fancied that the love of Socrates for Alcibiades was a mere sentimental addition to his philosophical reasonings, that a mere personal interest attaches to the one which must be kept as distinct as possible from that stern and severe method which he continually aimed at in the other. We think Proclus has very clearly shewn this conclusion, however just it might be if applied to Aristotle or Zeno, is entirely false in reference to his master. The chief obligation, if we are not mistaken,—and it is a very great one—which the disciple and admirer of Plato is under to this commentator, is that he has shewn the elenctic or dialec-

Our obligations to Proclus.

Harmony of love and science.

tical processes for which Socrates is so famous, to be connected by close and inseparable links not only with a moral purpose but with his affections. The value of his testimony and of his proofs on this point is greatly enhanced by the dryness and formality of his own disposition. His faculty is entirely of the logical kind. Here and there one may find a phrase, or even a sentence, which has a kind of poetical illumination in it; but it shines with an altogether reflected light, and one could scarcely imagine any one so continually in communication with Plato who has so little of vitality or of humour. His homage to Love, then, is a homage to Science. He may be quoted as the most satisfactory of witnesses to a truth which we believe all increased study of philosophical history will demonstrate more fully, that the highest science is not merely compatible with the most divine and most human love, but that they cannot exist apart. Admitting this as a result which is so important that Proclus or any man may well have been sent into the world to illustrate it, and that no fatigue should be grudged by the listeners which helps to fix it in their minds, we must yet remark that it is a very great effort to believe in Socrates or in Alcibiades, or in any living creatures at all, while we are perusing this most ingenious and elaborate commentary upon their relations to each other. The quintessence we have, no doubt, if it consists in refined disquisitions, or in the translation of human beings into the ideas which they embody. But if this is the best thing which the man can do for us who contains Orpheus, Plato, and Aristotle in himself, we should for our own parts be glad to have him reduced again into his original elements, and to get the very tiniest of them in place of the entire compound. If it is asked, then, whether we are content with the hints of a higher and purer love which these men of the old world give us, whether we do not want a Proclus to exhibit, even if it be in a less striking and vital form the complete ideal at which they are aiming ; if M. Cousin, or any of his disciples, will force these questions upon us, we must at all hazard of appearing very ridiculous in their eyes answer " We look for the Ideal of that which is personal in a person. We cannot understand either the pure affection of any man of the old world towards a disciple, or his zeal for truth, unless that affection and that zeal are more perfectly embodied than he exhibited then. It seems, therefore, to us that the effort of Proclus was to get rid of that which explains the mysteries of the old world, and to substitute for it a theory which is obliged to sustain itself by the traditions which that world found untenable. Proclus certainly has detected the secret principle which is implied in the dialogue of Alcibiades,

Proclus not imaginative.

Proclus a lover of abstractions.

Need of an ideal which shall not be an abstraction.

and more or less in all the Platonical dialogues. But he has left it as he found it, only adding to it a ponderous dæmonology, which, if it is true, demands the interpretation which the dialogues demand, and which, if true or false, affords no help to any mortal creature in becoming what Socrates and Plato would have him become."

Mixture of loyalty and slavery in Proclus.

10. We are fully aware that we shall be accused of leading our readers back into an old and customary rut when we venture remarks of this kind. But let those who dread ruts fairly give themselves to the study of Proclus; let them find, if they can, among all the slaves of tradition, one who bound himself so entirely to the yoke of a master as he did, one who so little dared to walk alone. We do not find fault with him for his addiction either to the old teacher or to the members of the sacred succession. Whatever there is good in him arises from his loyalty. He would be far less original than he is if he had trusted more to his native wit. By faithfully endeavouring to understand others, he rose by degrees into some strong and distinct convictions of his own; in trying to bring their thoughts together and present them to his class, he attained to some knowledge of what was going on in himself. Many may have gone through the same process. We have no right to pronounce it an illegitimate one. But for those who affect a particularly free habit of mind, and who scorn the fetters of the past, to take Proclus as their hero and guide, is the most surprising of all contradictions.

General dæmonology p. 182—212. Dæmon of Socrates, p. 212—232.

11. The passages in the commentary which refer to the dæmon of Socrates, though mixed of course with the later dæmonology of which Socrates knew nothing, are perhaps the most instructive in this part of the writings of Proclus, both historically and philosophically. We prefer, indeed, to take Socrates as the interpreter of his teachings and inspirations, and much of what Proclus says about the natural bias of the old Athenian towards good which made it necessary that he should have a power to restrain him, not one to urge him on, is to us unintelligible, and is quite inconsistent, we think, with his own statements. Still, the hints which the lecturer supplies on this topic serve very strikingly to connect the former with the later world, and suggest thoughts to each man respecting the government to which he is subjected, that should profit us more than they did his disciples. There are also observations strangely introduced, which, if they are not quite new, are nevertheless such as time can never make old. Thus, for instance, the mention of the crowd of lovers or admirers by whom Alcibiades was surrounded suggests the enquiry "What, then, is this crowd? Every one must see that it is a multitude, but a multitude undefined, con-

P. 213.
οὐκ ἐδεῖτο
τῆς αὑτοῦ
δαίμονος
προτροπῆς·
ὥρμητο γὰρ
ἀφ᾽ ἑαυτοῦ,
κ.τ.λ.

Political hints.

P. 157.

fused, unorganised. It is not a multitude in the sense in which a choir is a multitude, nor in which a people is. For a people is a multitude bound together within itself, but a crowd is a multitude merely consisting of loose elements. Hence it is commonly said that in politics ochlocracy differs from democracy, in that the one is out of measure and tune, the other is established under laws. Evidently, therefore, in this crowd, we have the tokens of a scattered dissipated life, one that draws down the object of its love into the material and divided and complex image of the different passions. Thus, Timæus called by this name all that which was reduced to no law of reason, the unmodulated and disorderly chaos that proceeded from the different elements of fire, and air, and earth, and water." Our readers, we hope, will discern something of an order emerging out of this chaos, and will admit that Proclus has made the most of the hint which Socrates has given him.

12. A far deeper subject, connected with all the thoughts of this time, and deserving the most careful attention of the historian, is brought before us in the following sentences. Proclus had been saying that Love cannot be reckoned among the highest or among the lowest classes of Beings. The reason given is that the thing loved (τὸ ἐραστὸν) must be beyond Love itself; but that Love cannot be severed from the Good or Beautiful, of which it participates; it is therefore not transcendant but mediatorial. He then proceeds—" In what, then, has it its first subsistence (ποῦ δὴ οὖν ὑπέστη τὴν πρώτην), and how goes it forth towards all things, and with what monads has it sprung out into activity? There being three substances (ὑποστάσεων) in the noetic and hidden gods; the first denoted by Goodness (τῷ ἀγαθῷ χαρακτηριζομένης) perceiving the essential Good, which is, as the oracle declares, the Paternal Monad (πατρικὴ μονάς); the second denoted by Wisdom (τὸ σοφὸν), in which dwells also the primary Intelligence (νόησις); the third denoted by the Beautiful (τὸ καλὸν). Corresponding to these noetic principles there subsist three monads, dwelling together, when contemplated as the principle or cause of noetic things in one form or kind; but first of all shining forth in the unspeakable order of the gods, as Faith, Truth, Love. Faith that establisheth all things, and settleth it in the Good; Truth that unfolds all the knowledge that is in any beings; Love that converteth all things, and draweth them into the nature of the Good. And this Triad proceedeth forth to all the orders of gods, and causeth the unity so to shine forth as to come within the scope of Intelligence; but in each order it has a different manifestation, uniting its own powers with the idiosyncrasies of the gods . . . . For all things, says the oracle, in' these three,

The Platonical Triad, p. 138—142.

Goodness, Wisdom, Love, the three Monads.

Passage from the Ineffable to the Intelligible.

124   THE GODS, ANGELS, HEROES, AND SYRIANUS.

are governed and are ; and for that reason the Gods command the Theurgists by these three to unite themselves to the God."

The discourses on the Parmenides, ed. Paris. Vol. 4.

13. We shall not stop now to comment on this passage, though we are not insensible to its importance as condensing the thoughts of many generations of Platonists on this subject, as supplying hints on philosophical and theological terminology, and as marking the differences and resemblances between the Christian and Platonical schools. But all these points will come more properly under our consideration hereafter, and in the meantime we must speak of that work to which Proclus himself and his disciple considered the lectures on the Alcibiades only the vestibule—his discourses on the Parmenides. What he thought of this task, when he entered upon it, may be judged from the solemn prayer with which the first book opens:

Opening invocation, p. 3—5.

—" I pray to all the gods and all the goddesses to guide my reason in the speculation which lies before me, and having kindled in me the pure light of truth, to direct my mind upwards to the very knowledge of the things that are, and to open the doors of my soul to receive the divine guidance of Plato, and having directed my knowledge into the very brightness of being, to withdraw me from the various forms of opinion, from the apparent wisdom, from the wandering about things that are not, by that purest intellectual exercise about the things that are, whereby alone the eye of the soul is nourished and

ἐνδῦναί τε μοι νοῦν μὲν τέλεον τοὺς νοητοὺς θεοὺς δύναμιν δ' ἀναγωγὸν τοὺς νοεροὺς.

brightened, as Socrates says in the Phædrus, and that the noetic gods will give to me the perfect nous, and the noeric gods the power that leads up to this, and that the rulers of the universe above the heaven will impart to me an energy unshaken by material notions and emancipated from them, and those to whom the world is given as their dominion a winged life, and the angelic choirs a true manifestation of divine things, and the good dæmons the fulness of the inspiration that comes from the gods, and the heroes a grand and venerable and lofty fixedness of mind, and the whole divine race together a perfect preparation for the participation in Plato's most mystical and far-seeing speculations, which he declares to us himself in the Parmenides with the profundity fitting such topics, but which he (i. e. his master Syrianus) completed by his own most pure and most luminous apprehensions, who did most truly share the

ὁ τῷ Πλάτωνι μὲν συμ- βακχεύσας ὡς ἀληθῶς, καὶ ὁ μεστὸς καταστὰς τῆς θείας ἀληθείας.

Platonic feast, and was the medium for transmitting the divine truth, and was the guide in our speculations and the hierophant of these divine words; who, I should say, came down as a type of philosophy of men to do good to the souls that are here, in place of images, sacrifices, the whole mystery of purification, a leader of salvation to the men that are now and that shall be hereafter. And may the whole band of those that are above us be propitious, and may the whole force that they supply be at hand, kindling before us the light which proceeding *from* them may guide us *to* them."

14. This somewhat inflated invocation, which will shew the reader what reverence the Athenian doctors bestowed upon each other, as well as upon the heroes and the choirs of angels, is still a satisfactory evidence that Proclus regarded the questions which philosophy raises with an awe which has been greatly wanting in some of its later professors. He was surely right in considering that when Parmenides spoke of the One, he must have had an awful sense that he was approaching the ground and root of things, an abyss deeper than his own spirit, one which that spirit could only contemplate when it had undergone a moral purification. He is certainly right that Socrates, young man as Plato represents him to have been when he conversed with Parmenides and Zeno, felt the dignity and dreadfulness of the enquiry in which they were engaged, though he did not shrink from courageously entering upon it himself, and though the object of his life was to clear a road by which others might travel in the same direction. And we cannot conceive that he was wrong in holding that each new student must tremble as much as his predecessors have done, confessing that he is on holy ground. It is the great redeeming point in Proclus, that while he looks upon the search for absolute unity as the search of the philosopher, he does not willingly reduce this unity into a dead abstraction, that he *tries* to identify it with a living Being. The effort is unspeakably difficult to him, for the Creator of the universe—and he fully admits a Creator of the universe—must, he thinks, be secondary and inferior to the one pure unutterable essence. To mix Him with his works or even with any working, is a kind of impiety. Hence, as we have seen in the preliminary invocation, and as we found was the case with the author of the Mysteries, the primitive and eternal Nous soars above all the efficient and energising gods; a vision of supreme goodness rises above even that; a transcendant unity is still perceivable through this goodness. Through tiers of beings does the poor overwhelmed seeker ascend towards this distant effulgence; or is it an opaque substance from which all effulgence has departed? And the while he feels as if this mysterious unity could not be far from him, as if it were implied in all he speaks and does, as if it were pre-supposed in the multitude of things which his eye beholds, still more in every act of his mind when he thinks of those things. He feels also as if the absolute and eternal One must in a direct and mysterious way be acting upon him, and as if there must be

Reverence of Proclus.

His great difficulty.

some nearer passage to it than through those orders of beings who, howsoever his intellect may arrange and compose them, introduce plurality into his thoughts, and disturb his efforts to dwell in a region that is above it. We will frankly own, that if we had not travelled this road before with Augustin, and had not learnt by what a painful and practical method he was led to behold the absolute Good, the absolute One, as inseparable from a Person in whom he lived, and moved, and had his being, if we had not learnt how he found in Whom this Unity and Goodness might be approached and apprehended, these enquiries of Proclus would seem to us utterly interminable, full of the profoundest interest and the profoundest despair, each step involving a new contradiction, with the perpetual fear that if the mists ever should disperse, and the different forms which perplexed the vision while it was beset by them disappear, nothing would remain but vacancy. When the Commentary is read along with the Confessions, a light falls on it; all the hints of a philosophical method whereby a man may disengage himself from the phantoms of sense, and begin to see things as they are, to recognise a unity in them, to see a unity above and beyond them, for which Proclus is indebted to Socrates, promise to become practically helpful. The Theurgy which was derived from his own immediate masters, is translated from a vague, half believed superstition, necessary to fill up the blanks in philosophy, into a divine science which is at the root of it, and which quickens it. Even the pettinesses and paltrinesses of the sage give us a kind of interest in him, as witnesses that he shared our frailties, and that a complete system never shall be wrought out in God's living universe, which shall not betray its own feebleness, and let in the light and air of heaven through a thousand cracks and fissures.

<small>Augustin and Proclus. The highest vision of Unity and Good won through the experience of sorrow and evil.</small>

<small>Proclus according to Morbeka.</small> 15. There are three treatises by Proclus, the original of which is lost, but of which the substance is preserved in a Latin translation by a Corinthian Archbishop of the twelfth century. For the easy and tolerably flowing Greek of the Athenian scholar we have the uncouth version of a man who was trying to render philosophical thoughts into a language which he imperfectly understood, and which he must have considered more unfit for the purpose than it actually was. Yet we have the bad taste to think these on the whole the most valuable compositions which Proclus has bequeathed to us; valuable partly for the very cause which makes the reading of them painful. Merely to a philologer, the spectacle of a Greek struggling to find Latin equivalents for his words, or when that task is hopeless, giving them Latin terminations, is amusing and not unin-

structive. But to the historian of philosophy, who is about very Value of the shortly to leave the original home of science, where all the translation, ed. Paris, finest shades and distinctions of thought and speculation Vol. 1. had become familiar and conventional, to see a set of hardy Latinised Goths awakening to a new world of invisible things, and trying to make the visible world which they were subduing with sword and ploughshare, furnish them with instruments for expounding the secrets of it, books are of immense value which connect the perishing cultivation with the fresh and hopeful barbarism. Morbeka's translation serves this purpose. And as the works with which he has presented us are not lectures, And of the but letters or essays, Proclus appears less in the character of a Treatises themselves. verbal critic; his worship of Plato does not afford him the same excuse for endless gossiping. Not that Plato is ever forgotten. In the opening of the second of his treatises on Providence, he Etenim boldly affirms that the preservation of the sacred Platonical hanc ipsam oraculorum oracles, and the handing down of them from age to age, through traditionem ad dignos a series of worthy auditors, is itself a demonstration of Provi- Deorum dence, were others wanting. At the same time he declares with auditores æstimo esse much truth, as we have already intimated, that the study of aper- Plato had awakened and not stifled his self-reflection, and that tissimam Providentiæ Mercury being their common teacher, it signified little whether demonstra- the words had been first uttered by the ancients or elaborated tionem, &c. p. 91. by himself.

16. The first of these treatises is "On Providence and Fate, Opinion of and that which is in us;" the second resolves ten doubts about Theodorus. P. 10, § 2. Providence; the third treats of the subsistence of evil things. *Theodorus*, to whom the first of these treatises is addressed, had adopted a theory of the universe which he was certainly not the first or the last to maintain. Looking at the various tragical and comical connections of human events, he supposed them to Hanc Provi- dentiam be held together by a certain mechanical law or fate. This he hymnizasti ut solum- was disposed to call Providence, and to endue with free-will. modo But that which is called free-will in man, he rejected as merely αὐτεξούσιον. Humanæ nominal and imaginary. Fate, then, and Providence differed autem according to Theodorus, in that the first expressed a series of animæ vulgatum antecedents and consequents, the latter the necessity which pro- αὐτεξούσιον duces these. Proclus, on the contrary, proposes to show, 1st. nomen solum esse. That Fate and Providence are both causes of the world, and of Ambo the things which come to pass in the world, but that Providence quidem is antecedent to Fate, that all things which happen according to causas mundi et Fate come to pass by a much earlier law from Providence, but eorum quæ that the converse is not true, for that the whole order of things in mundo fiunt, esse, depending directly on Providence, is diviner than Fate. præexistere 2nd. That there is one soul which is separable from the body, autem Pro- videntiam

and comes down from above from the gods into this mortal sphere; that there is another dwelling in bodies which cannot be separated from the things that are lying about it and beneath, that the latter indeed depends upon Fate, but the other upon Providence, in virtue of its own substance. 3d. That there is one kind of knowledge and truth in souls brought under the law of generation and birth, even though they be spotless in life, another to those who fly from this mortal sphere and have established themselves in that place whence they first fell and descended hither. If these distinctions are fully recognised, he thinks that all the difficulties of the subject will be cleared away. It will be evident in what wise many things escape Fate, but Providence nothing. It will be evident from the second proposition, how truly there is a free-will in that principle which is within us, but how when this obeys necessity, and is led by Fate, its freedom becomes languid and dead, in consequence of an evil life, though it still participates in a certain phantom of choice in virtue of the better soul which is its neighbour. From the third position we discover what Parmenides, Socrates, and Plato meant when they said that the soul, after it is purged from earthly passions and mixtures, may even here perceive truth, and will enjoy a nobler and purer science after it has been released the laws of birth and matter.

17. Our readers will not be surprised that Proclus should devote his chief diligence to the illustration of the second of these principles, or that the really valuable part of his treatise should be that which treats of the principle *in us*—that which is immediately under the divine direction, which is free while it acknowledges that direction, which becomes slavish by acknowledging itself merely as a part of nature, and therefore subject to necessity, and yet which can never lose the tokens of a higher origin and life. We must express our gratitude to him for having untied with great dexterity some of the knots in this most difficult and interesting of all questions: untied them, we mean, so far as to make the logical statement of the problems of human life more precise and clear. The problems themselves have to be worked out by other aid, and under other guidance, than that which he can afford us; but *quod dat accipimus*, not without some shame for having perhaps undervalued other presents of his by which we might have profited.

17. The ten Doubts on Providence have been in most of our minds, and on the greater part of them Proclus has something to say which is worth listening to. The first (*a*) is, whether Providence takes account of all things, of wholes, of parts, even down to the most individual things in the heavens and under

the heavens, eternal things and corruptible. The second (b) (b) 98—100. is, whether Providence takes cognisance of contingencies. The third (c), if Providence is the cause both of things determinate (c) 100—116. and things indeterminate. Is it the cause of both in the same way or in a different way? The fourth (d), is on the question (d) 116—123. how it is possible to participate in the nature of the gods. The fifth (e) is the more terrible question, how evil can have (e) 123—131. place among beings while there is a Providence. The sixth (f) (f) 131—144. concerns the inequality of the lives of men in the universe. The seventh (g) refers to the differences of condition in inani- (g) 144—153. mate creatures apparently not susceptible of moral evil. The eighth (h), refers to the delay of punishments and the apparent (h) 153—168. disconnection between crime and punishment. The ninth (i), (i) 168—174. is on the question how the evils of one generation can be visited upon another. The tenth (k) is in what sense, seeing that Pro- (k) 174—179. vidence has been connected with the unity and with the perfect good, angels, and dæmons, and heroes, can be said to exercise it. The statement of these difficulties may shew us with what awful questionings of the human spirit the Neo-Platonist was willing to engage. Are we to mourn that he did not provide us with formulas for the settlement of them which could save us from the necessity of encountering them ourselves?

18. The questions mooted in the third treatise are these. Third treatise, Whether Evil is or not. If it is, whether in things intellectual p. 197. or not. If in things sensible, whether in virtue of that which is their original cause. If not, whether substance is in any wise to be ascribed to it, or it is to be set down as wholly unsubstantial. If it has subsistence, in what wise it subsists, and whither it tends : how, there being a Providence, Evil is and whence it is. On all these points he says, and before all, he must adhere to the doctrine of Plato ; he can do nothing Nihil if he departs from him. As we have already made copious reputabimur tractasse extracts from the book of Plotinus which refers to this subject, nobis ab we shall not trouble our readers with a discussion proceeding illius theoriâ deci- from what, in spite of M. Cousin, we must consider an infe- dentibus, rior mind. Both sages arrive at the same conclusion. The p. 198. following passage will perhaps assist us as much in understanding the object and the result of the treatise as any we could select. "Of all things it would seem to be the most difficult to know the nature of Evil in itself, seeing that all knowledge P. 273—274, is the knowledge of species or form. But Evil is without § 5. form, and, so to speak, privation. Perhaps, however, we may arrive at some satisfaction on this point, too, by contemplating Good in itself, and the nature of things which are good. For as the primary good is beyond and above all things, so Evil in itself is that which is divested of all

good. In so far forth as it is evil, it is the defect and privation of this. In what wise Good subsists, and what degrees it has, has been set forth elsewhere. But Evil, as Evil, is that which is separated from the fountain of Good; separated in so far as it is objectless and vague from the primary object; in so far as it is weakness, from the power which dwells in that object; in so far as it is want of harmony, falsehood, or baseness, from beauty and truth, and that by which things are united; in so far as it is restless and unstable from the abiding and eternal unity; in so far as it is privation and unvitality, from the first Monad and the life which is in it; in so far as it tends to corrupt, and divide, and make imperfect, the things with which it hath to do, from the goodness which is bringing the universe to perfection. For the corruptive draws from that which is to that which is not; the divisive destroys the continuity and union of being; the imperfect takes from each thing the perfection and order which belongs to its own nature."

Injustitiam ipsam secundùm se debilem et inactivam esse ait; justitiæ autem præsentiâ et potentiam habere et ad agere duci non manentem in sui ipsius naturâ, neque in ἀζωία privatione solùm, quoniam et præjacens ipsum vitale ens dat et malo vitæ participationem, p. 276.

He goes on to explain with considerable skill and subtlety, though confessing that all he says has been said before by Plato, how that which is evil and unjust while in itself it is only negative, yet derives a kind of positiveness and reality from the presence of the goodness and justice to which it is opposed. And thus it is intelligible how might should belong essentially to right, and be inseparable from it; the very power which seems to belong to wrong being in fact derived from the fellowship of that which it is weakening and undermining.

19. With this precious moral truth upon his lips we take a friendly farewell of Proclus. The parting is somewhat more solemn, because, as our readers must have gathered from our previous remarks, it is not from a man merely but from a period. Whatever be the merits or the defects of this Platonical teacher, it is with him the Greek philosophy, as such, closes its records. We do not mean that he left no successors. It was in the next century, not in this, that the Athenian schools were closed. But it had done whatever it had to do when Proclus delivered his last lecture. Our friend the Corinthian Archbishop, in his barbarous Latin-Greek lingo, signifies to us that whatever had been once spoken in the proper tongue of the wise men, must undergo a transformation before it could live again. And, therefore, we must stand still for a moment, though we have studied the different parts of the landscape with some care, that we may consider it as a whole before it vanishes from us.

Proclus practically the last of an age.

Recapitulation.

20. We spoke in the former part of this treatise of the Platonical dialogues as treating of *Being*, or that which is and which may be detected amidst all the confused appearances of things; of *Ideas*, which could neither be said to exist in the

thinker nor in that of which he thinks, which are substantial, not forms of our minds though implied in all the forms of our minds, not subject to the conditions of time and of space but unchangeable and eternal; finally, of *Unity*, or *the One* which is implied in all the thoughts of man, in the arrangements and existence of human society, in the order of the visible universe. We pointed out why, as it seemed to us, Plato had been least successful in handling this last subject, most profound and instructive when he was treating of that Unity which the politician is obliged to recognise and assume, and that which the dialectician seeks after when he is examining what is implied in the discourse and reasonings of man. In these two cases he was starting from data which his own experience and the experience of his country furnished him with; he was proceeding in a safe, cautious, experimental method, to discover what principles lay beneath facts which could not be gainsayed. In the other case he was starting from hypotheses, he was considering how the world might have been formed; he had not yet learnt how to question its phenomena and to extract from them their law, as he questioned those which had to do directly with himself and with mankind. Hence, we said, it had come to pass that the Timæus, though the great armoury for those who wish to make out a system of Platonical opinions, is the worst guide of all to the Platonical philosophy, which is nothing else than a method of emancipation from Platonical opinions and all other opinions,—a search after a ground of reality that lies beneath all opinions.

Platonical subjects. See Part I. art. Plato.

21. Now, if we are asked how far this philosophy was pursued by the spiritual descendants of Plato—how far a Platonical system was substituted for it—we have endeavoured in several particular cases to indicate the answer. The pursuit after Being, or that which is, in the Socratic sense and Socratic method, was, we have remarked, abandoned by Plotinus not entirely, for he was a self-questioner, but to a very great extent because he had none of the practical habits of Socrates, none of his sympathy with common life. When the Iamblichan theurgy permanently established itself in fellowship with his more pure philosophy, there was no doubt a greater mixture of the popular element with the philosophical; but it was just that popular element of which Socrates was trying to get rid, just that which checked his own pursuit after the reality of things. The reader is not at first aware how much this is the case, because he finds Socratic phrases, respecting the things that are and the things that are not, continually in the mouths of the mythological doctors, and because he finds as frequent allusions to mythological fables in the Platonical dialogues themselves as

The τὸ ὄν

The abstract and the popular.

IDEAS BECOMING ACTUAL

The inquirer and the lecturer.

in their commentaries. But if he looks carefully, he will observe this most striking difference, that Socrates is feeling his way to a substantial truth through the story, that the others are trying to justify or reconstruct the story merely as the vehicle or instrument for enunciating some principle. Proclus, it may be admitted, is less busy in this work than some of the more polemical teachers of the preceding century. His intense and slavish addiction to Plato, and his want of imagination, make him prefer the dry letter to the ornamental illustration. But it cannot be said that he comes nearer to the simplicity of Socrates when he forsakes the declamatory style. He is always the lecturer who lays down principles, never the free and friendly inquirer who is working them out.

Ideas.

22. The next department of the Platonical philosophy, that which we spoke of as belonging more to the disciple than to the master, to the profound thinker than to the homely questioner, the doctrine of Ideas, is one on which the New Platonists believed that they had especial illumination. They thought that *How treated by the new school.* if Ideas were, as Plato said, substantial, not mere notions of our minds, they must come to us in some real actual form; they must come forth from the primary substance, and present themselves to us. Thus the Platonic Ideas or Ideals are transformed into that host of spiritual persons, secondary Gods, Angels, Dæmons, Heroes, Souls, which are everywhere flitting before us in the writings of the later doctors. You are never quite certain what guise these personages may put on. You are listening to Syrianus or Proclus in his chair; it is a world of Ideas to which you are introduced, ideas immeasurably less substantial than those with which one has been familiar in Plato's own writings. But the professor has slipped off his cloak, and has clothed himself in the robes which become him as priest of the *Their uncertainty.* universe. In a moment the ideas have been converted into living creatures, mediators between the transcendant Unity and the human sage still mixing with the clods of earth. We are far from wishing to impute this apparent uncertainty as a crime to the new school. We have stated already why we believe it was inevitable. If Plato's statement of the law under which man perceives that which is absolute and eternal is the true one, if any conception which we form of the absolute Essence must be idolatrous and imperfect because it is our conception, if yet the spirit of man is created to receive the knowledge of this highest Essence, and must receive it in order that it may reach its highest blessedness, the Platonist can never have been content until the divine Ideal proved itself not to be *Necessity of a dæmonology.* the work of his intellect or imagination, and yet proved itself to have the most intimate relation with both, with his very

self. Either philosophical anticipations had nothing corresponding to them in reality, which Plato assumes that they must have, or this anticipation must meet some time or other its counterpart. And then how would it be possible to go on merely speaking of the Ideal? The New-Platonist said that when the Christian church talked of the divine Ideal as manifested, they talked nonsense. The only sense that could be substituted for that nonsense was that in which Julian, Iamblichus, and Proclus so firmly believed.

23. The subject of Unity, in so far as it has to do with dialectics,—that is to say in so far as the question is by what process man may obtain to the knowledge of the pure and absolute Unity, has been spoken of already in our remarks upon the Parmenides, as treated by Proclus. That the necessity of such a Unity had become more obvious to the commentator, even than it was to the master, is sufficiently evident. That a mere abstract Unity, apart from a living Being, was a vision from which the elder sage revolted, which the later felt to be impossible, we have joyfully confessed. That Proclus had even more difficulty than Plato in reconciling his conviction with the fact, we have been obliged to admit. By some means or other the belief of a One living ground of man and of the universe had established itself and got root. The philosopher did willing, but somewhat perplexed, homage to a truth which was sweeping a whole world before it; though the philosopher was shewing at the selfsame time how much he resembled the crowd in its unwillingness to abandon that old world, in its readiness to rebuild its idolatries upon a new foundation. *Unity dialectical.*

24. But if the unity of the Parmenides was partially asserted by the new school, what could they do to assert the unity of the Republic? Proclus could see the difference between a democracy and ochlocracy. Old Athenian wisdom served him so far. But could the great speculator on all human things throw the least light upon the question how men of different races, tribes, languages, might be one? how the divine pattern in the heavens which Plato saw might be a kingdom for the groaning and starving myriads upon earth? Not one syllable upon this subject, we do not say which could be intelligible to ignorant multitudes, but which could guide the thoughts of the man who believed in a higher destiny for his kind, and was willing to suffer with it, came forth from the sages of Athens or Alexandria, who proclaimed each other to be inspired. If what they said was true, a multitude of divine words had been spoken upon this earth, but nothing ever had been upon it for its deliverance. Gods noetic and noeric, *Unity political.* *The great failure.*

134 POLITICS; PHYSICS.

dæmons, heroes and divine souls, had all taken a mighty interest in some of its inhabitants; and it was hastening on to the abyss. We do not, indeed, deny that the earnest and instructive discourses of Proclus on the subject of evil, have a very direct bearing upon political life. The principle which he asserts that that which is one is good, that evil breaks, divides, disperses, contains within it the great maxim of social order, the indication of the causes which interrupt it, the encouragement to all hope in those who seek after it. But why was so precious a truth so ineffective a one? Where was the living uniting power that could hold society in one, despite of the power—apparent power it might only be in the eyes of the philosopher, but tremendously real for those who were crushed by it—that was ever threatening to tear it in pieces? Who could tell men of this, and where it dwelt? If not, what is the use of settling, even in the most satisfactory manner, whether Evil is or is not?

Valuable hint as to social life.

25. The unity of Nature was still left. The Timæus could supply plentiful theories to those who had never found the Atlantis of which it speaks. Proclus, we are told, wrote against the Mosaic account of the creation. Christian priests and Christian emperors, with their accustomed folly, wished to confute or to silence him. They represented, it would seem, that he believed in the eternity of the world, or that he confounded it with its Author. The charge is not true. We have given our readers proof enough out of his writings, in extracts certainly not selected for the purpose of glorifying him, which positively confute it. There was nothing in the tenour or habit of his speculations which inclined him to invest matter with any glory; everything which inclined him to disparage it. And though, like Plotinus, he carefully distinguished the Cosmos from matter, this had never the divinity in his mind which it had in the speculations of the Stoics. At the same time it was absolutely impossible for Proclus to understand Moses. The resemblance which Numenius had discovered between him and Plato had become every day since less visible to the school; the Hebrew had become more hopelessly untranslatable into the Attic. For the facts of light and darkness, of the firmament above and below, of earth and sea, of sun and moon, of birds, beasts, fishes, of man and woman, are those in which Moses finds his order, and which he refers directly to the creative Word; man being in the nearest relation to it. The simple institution of the week, with its day of rest and its days of work, is to the Jew the expression of God's rest and work, of man's rest and work,—of the relation of God to man, and of man to the world. Such an interpretation of the actual universe, as it presents itself to the eye of every peasant, such an assertion

Unity in the Cosmos.

Moses and Proclus.

that the highest God is providing for the ordinary wants of every peasant, and claiming him as the inheritor of the most mysterious blessings, was of course utterly vulgar and intolerable to a great theological cosmogonist who had discovered a multitude of other links and gradations between the divine and the human, the heavenly and the earthly. And how could a priest of the universe like Proclus, who was to eclecticise and harmonise all mythologies, endure the stern Jew who called upon all nations to confess the Lord of a few Syrian outcasts as their king? *The Jew and the Greek.*

26. Was it then because the Church was becoming specially Hebrew in its character in the fifth century, that it could not endure the contact of Neo-Platonism, and that the struggle between them was approaching its final crisis? Apparently there was no time in which the Hebrew characteristics were becoming weaker, or were more threatening to disappear. In *their* character of priests of the universe, the bishops and doctors of the Christian Church were practically admitting the old mythological notions to come and dwell within it, as the Platonists were incorporating them in their philosophy. Nor can it be said that they were less busy with hypotheses about the universe, with cosmogonical theories, than their opponents. The text of Moses was rigidly adopted; but it was overlaid with inferences and speculations which destroyed all its character, and made it just as artificial, just as far off from facts, as the Timæus, or as the Hindoo Puranas. But if the document was disguised, the institution which was the true commentary upon it had become a part of the life and order of Christendom. Moreover, men did wake in the morning to the perception that there was day, and were reminded, before twenty-four hours were at an end, that there was night. Summer and winter, seed-time and harvest, were discovered to be parts of the economy of life. And therefore plain people acknowledged a tie between them and the old narrative, and left the doctors to settle their questions as they liked. The Church was Hebraic in spite of itself. It was trying to construct a religion and a philosophy which should expel all other religions and philosophies, and should make the thoughts and inquiries of men needless or sinful. It was, in fact, standing on the proclamation of a one living God, who had created the universe, had revealed Himself to man, and who was awakening man to thoughts, aspirations, and hopes which would have been equally crushed if the patriarchs or the philosophers of Alexandria, of Constantinople, or of Athens, had been able to establish their dominion. *The Church not Hebrew in its speculations* *but Hebrew by necessity of their position.*

27. It is necessary to press these remarks upon our readers at this time, though we may have hinted them often before, lest

The Church victory no occasion for triumph. the fall of the schools of Neo-Platonism should awaken any shout of triumph among Churchmen, as if they had succeeded in treading down a dangerous adversary; or lest philosophers should complain that some great and hideous injustice was committed, or some great loss sustained by the universe. There is no cause for shouting among Churchmen: first, because no true principle which Platonism had asserted could by possibility die, no vital distinction which it had proclaimed could be effaced, though all the statesmen and the Churchmen in the universe should conspire to produce such a result. There *had* been true principles asserted by Plato: if they were forgotten or buried under theological theories, theologians in later days would have to seek them again, and reassert them as the justification of the facts and promises of the Gospel. There *were* vital distinctions established by Platonism,—the distinctions between the eternal and the temporal, the spiritual and the sensual, heaven and earth: if these were denied or made light of by Christian doctors, the humble members of the Christian Church would have to demand them again, that St. Paul and St. John might not be accused of deceiving them,—that they might not be robbed of treasures for which none that can be weighed in earthly balances are any compensation. And, such a shout of triumph over a fallen foe is most idle and uncalled for, because the confusions and perplexities of the Platonical school, and the phantasies and superstitions which overwhelmed it, belong to human nature. We shall have to trace the reappearance of them, under different forms, in all periods. The Christian doctor and priest is not more safe from them than another man. If he does not notice the forms which they have taken, and supposes that they belong to others, not to him, he will certainly fall into them.

The fall of Platonism no cause for lamentation. 28. But the philosophical dirge is as little reasonable as the ecclesiastical pæan. The work which Platonism had to do in the world, it had accomplished. If philosophers wish for a recognition of its worth from those whom they suppose are its enemies, the Christian literature of four centuries will supply it. If we compare Athanasius or Augustin with those who worshipped their names in later days, we shall know how, consciously or unconsciously, they were helped by Plato to do a work which their successors could not have done. And if this is not the kind of homage which the modern admirers of Plato would desire, they may trace through all the history of the time, indications how much the thoughts of which he was the utterer were at work in minds which knew nothing of him,— how much Society was receiving its outward character and form from certain great spiritual principles that could only be expressed in language speaking of Being, of Unity, of a human and divine Ideal. If these principles present themselves in history not as abstract forms, but as living facts, this is certainly what Socrates and Plato would have expected. This explains why the former clung so tenaciously to the wood of the carpenter and the last of the shoemaker; why the latter could ask even a tyrant of Syracuse to find himan actual world in which he might work, that he might escape from the abstractions which he hated.

29. If indeed Plato had been the only teacher of the old Greek world who had worked out important principles, or discovered a valuable method,—if there was no region besides the one to which he pointed the way—there might be some reason in the complaint that it could not last beyond the fifth or sixth century, and that a Church which had its foundation in Palestine, and received its lore from Semitic teachers, extinguished that which interfered with their supremacy. But we have always maintained that the field of thought in which Aristotle worked is one which requires and rewards cultivation, as well as that which his master tilled. Each, we have contended, in opposition to the pretensions of their respective schools, did what the other could not do. The disciples of Plato made him the systematiser which he was trying not to be, when they sought to bring the universe under his government. The great danger of Aristotle arose from the encyclopædic character of his mind, which made him suppose that he had comprehended all things because he had succeeded in discovering the formulas under which man conceives of all things. The proximate cause of the ruin of the Neo-Platonic school was that they fancied they could include Orpheus, Plato, Aristotle, in themselves,—that the universe had been in travail for nearly 5000 years only to bring them forth. If they were good Platonists, they could not be also good Aristotelians. They might honour Aristotle sincerely and profoundly, but it was mere arrogance to pretend that they could deal with the class of facts which he understood better than any man, upon their method. It was all very well for Cicero to unite the Academician and the Peripatetic. Mere artificial schools may always be accommodated, though they cannot be reconciled. But in the history of the world philosophies will either go for nothing, or they will prove their worth by connecting themselves with some distinct region of human experience which is demanding interpretation. We often hear of a tyranny of Aristotle which succeeded to the tyranny of Plato. Such language may have an important truth in it which we shall have to examine and to confess. But a tyranny does not establish itself for centuries upon an earth which is subject to an order, by mere accident. A man who has been in his grave a thousand

Why Plato could not be regarded as the philosopher.

Philosophical tyrannies —what they signify.

138   A CRISIS AT HAND.

<small>Aristotle.</small> years does not, in despite of a multitude of living obstacles, spring to a throne over the most thinking minds for a series of ages, merely because they have a mad propensity for being in bondage. It is not that propensity, but the desire for deliverance, for illumination, upon subjects on which darkness is intolerable and unsafe, which has led men to seek for one or another guide to their footsteps. We must understand through what path they were travelling, what the surrounding atmosphere was, before we can pronounce that they chose amiss. It may be that their temporary chief is the very one that has been appointed for them; that it would have been as perilous for them to have been without him, as it was to follow him, when they entered a new track which he had not trodden, or in which he had gone astray.

<small>Indications of a new epoch.</small> 30. Before the fifth century closed, there were very clear indications of the approach not of an Aristotelian school but of an Aristotelian epoch. We will point out in what direction these traces are to be sought. But when we have done our duty to chronology, by denoting the man who was to be the commencement of the new period, we shall reserve the consideration of his thoughts, which were to have so great an influence upon it, till it has actually commenced. <small>Bœthius, A. D. 470-524.</small> *Bœthius* is commonly spoken of as the swan from whose throat the dying notes of old classical eloquence proceeded; as the man who preserved the tradition of the age of Cicero, or at least of Pliny, in the days of the Ostrogoth. That honour may doubtless belong to him, and it is the one on which the scholar is most likely to dwell. The cruel sentence of the hitherto just ruler, upon the Roman Senator, the fact that he occupied his prison hours in writing the "Consolations of Philosophy," that, Christian as he was, he clung to that word as fondly as Augustin had done, the somewhat pedantical attachment with which he held by the old forms of the republic, like <small>The place assigned him by scholars.</small> the Arnolds and Rienzis of after days, offer a sufficient excuse for that classification which connects him with the world that had been, rather than with that which was to be. But those who love to watch the birth more than the death of things—who welcome Theodoric's government as the sign that a modern Europe was bursting from a shell which it had taken 500 years to break—have a right to claim the honourable name of his victim as most properly belonging to them. As Englishmen we might insist that when Saxon and Roman wisdom first began to mingle and understand each other under the auspices of Alfred, the "Consolations of Philosophy" was chosen to express their union, or the transition from one to the other. But the student of the history of European philosophy is under a much stronger obligation not to treat Bœthius as a mere relic of the past.

The continual references to him in the Middle Ages are not chiefly to his ethics but much more to his logic. It is in his character as a logical writer that he shews what the tendencies of the coming time were, with what kind of questions it would be occupied. Augustin, Latin as he was, is emphatically the Latin *Platonist*: his divinity, as much as his philosophy, is conversant with the eternal, and with man's relations to it. The forms in which men speak and reason are interesting to him only as he contemplates them from this higher ground. Böethius on the contrary is the Latin *Aristotelian*, and the one who showed how much more naturally the Latin mind, when left to itself, and out of the reach of Greek influences, sympathises with the Aristotelian than with the Platonic temper. Under what modifications this is true, to what apparent and to what real exceptions it is liable, to what degree other influences besides the purely Latin were at work in the Middle Ages, how the Gothic, the Hebrew, the Arabic, the purely Christian influences conspired or counteracted each other, these are questions which we shall have to consider hereafter. And that we may consider them more satisfactorily, we hasten to conclude our narrative of the properly Greek school, by glancing at the events of the sixth century, which was to prepare the way for the future philosophy of Europe, though it may have supplied no names on which it behoves us to dwell.

He occupies a different one in philosophical history.

The Latin Aristotelian.

CHAPTER VI.

The Sixth Century.

1. We said that no great philosophical names would cause us to linger over the records of the Sixth Century. There are two unphilosophical names which every one recollects who thinks of it: perhaps we may have more to say of these than of many who have founded schools and composed systems. They are both of them far more memorable for what they did by themselves, or through others, than for what they thought; yet they have both, consciously or unconsciously, affected speculation as much as action. When they sought to hinder or direct its course, their movements were often feeble, sometimes mischievous, and ultimately led to results which they did not foresee and might have wished to avert. But a mightier power than their own was using them as instruments in building up the social and spiritual life of Christendom, as well as in preparing the way for its greatest disruption. We speak of the Emperor Justinian and the Pope Gregory I.

The leading men of the Sixth Century.

140 CONSTANTINOPLE IN GLORY.

Justinian. 2. The life of Justinian is directly connected with our subject, inasmuch as it was his decree which closed for ever the lips of those Athenian teachers with whom we were so much occupied in the last chapter. But after the remarks which we made on the waning of Neo-Platonism even in its great representative, Proclus, and on the evident tokens which his writings furnished that it had fully delivered its message to mankind, this event, taken by itself, would not seem to be of any great importance. Romulus Augustulus stands as the representative of the death of an empire, and the moment of its extinction has a certain solemnity in it; but we feel that it was doomed, and only wonder that it lasted so long. To know exactly when the *The outward and inward history of his reign connected.* last Platonist of the Empire fled from it to try his fortune in another region, is not uninteresting; but the interest is rather sentimental than practical. If, therefore, this had been a solitary act of the Emperor; if the rest of his doings, though apparently most unconnected with it, had not been a commentary upon it, and had not received illustration from it; we might have passed it by with a very casual notice. But there is no great transaction of this memorable reign; no proceeding of the monarch, however paltry as to the motive in which it originated, or its immediate object; no war that was waged with other nations; no striving in the Church, or the Circus of Constantinople; which has not a clear internal relation to this decree, and which is not, like this, an index to the moral and intellectual condition of a period.

The legislator. 3. If we contemplate Justinian in that aspect in which his panegyrists would like best to exhibit him, as the man at whose bidding Tribonian and his associates compiled the Institutes, the Pandects, and the Code, we discover the character of his reign and the kind of influence which it was to exercise. Considering that this was the time in which Constantinople most pretended to dominion over the world,—most vindicated the *Bows to Latin wisdom.* design of its founder, by proving itself to be *the* Capital,—one cannot but be struck with the strange fact, that just then the Greek should have paid the profoundest and most permanent homage to the Latin wisdom. There is, no doubt, mixed in the *Corpus* a certain Greek element; but how weak and inconsiderable compared with the contributions of the old jurists of the Roman world; how clearly they prove *their* language to be the one that was fittest for expounding rights and obligations; the function of their race to be that of organising bodies of men, of ascertaining by what covenants and contracts they are held to each other, of fixing the method and limits of punishment! Justinian's compilation is the most frank and childlike confession of this superiority,—a declaration that Constantinople could only govern the world through the influences bequeathed to it by that city which seemed no longer capable of governing itself, scarcely of maintaining its existence.

4. It would be sufficiently clear from this document, were there no other facts to sustain it, that this treasure had passed to heirs who, even when they possessed it, could not use it. Laws might be adopted or enacted by a Greek Emperor, but he did not know wherein their force lay: he fancied they proceeded from his own will: that which had established itself by centuries of struggle between opposing wills,—which could control, as long as anything could, the wild impulses of Italian tyrants and Italian legions,—seemed to the Byzantine the creature of his own despotism. He had not even skill to hide the contradiction from his subjects; still less had he skill to inspire them with any settled reverence either for edicts written in letters, or for the person who sanctioned them. The volatile mob of his Capital was never more prone to tumults, more impatient of authority, than under the man who clothed himself with the justice of foregone centuries, and assumed that it proceeded from his mouth.

The Emperor did not know whence the force of laws is derived.

5. But it was not only to the Rome of other days that Constantinople, in the person of Justinian, paid obeisance. His predecessors, like so many of his successors, maintained the dignity of the Patriarchs, as well as that of the Empire, against the spiritual authority which a series of strange events was making the only one in the old city of the Cæsars. Justinian appearing to have a mightier empire than any Byzantine monarch had ever enjoyed, confessed the dominion of the Popes when it looked most weak and in the greatest peril. For them he legislated, for them he conquered. By whatever means they had won their authority, he felt it to be more substantial than his own, for it was establishing itself over the minds and hearts of men of various tribes, and these, even within his very palace, proved refractory to him.

His homage to the Popes.

6. No doubt there were strong and obvious motives which influenced the monarch in taking this course. The immediate opposition was greater in his eyes than the distant one: Greek and Egyptian bishops, or (if these could be tamed by Court favours)—monks, might be a more perilous disturbance to his power than an Italian bishop could ever be. If he could secure their allegiance by enlisting a ruler on his side whom they would honour because he was ecclesiastical, however they might be offended at him because he was Latin, the concession of a nominal supremacy would be a cheap sacrifice. So Justinian probably argued with himself: the frightful consequences of theological controversies to some recent Emperors added the greatest practical weight to the reasoning. But the policy of

Policy of this obedience.

Justinian was determined by causes far mightier than his powers of seeing or foreseeing. He was yielding to a hidden force which he could not control. He submitted to the Papal ascendancy, for he had no might in his own world which could be matched against it.

Conquests of Justinian. 7. And yet it seemed as if the hosts which Belisarius led into Africa and Italy, and which effected such triumphs there, had a might like that which once belonged to the legions of Pompey or of Trajan. The nature and consequences of these victories concern our subject more nearly than we might at first fancy. The death-bed of Augustin was saddened, his faith called forth, *Defeat of the Arians in Africa.* by the news that Hippo was besieged by the Vandals through the crime of his friend Boniface. From that time the Arians had been rulers of the African province; the believers in the Trinity had been exposed to the cruelest persecutions. Justinian sent forth his troops more to put down heretics than to win new provinces for the Empire. The work was a complete one: the Vandals were exterminated. The temporary rule of Constantinople was connected with the reappearance of an indigenous African population. The most signal victory of the Cross, as it appeared to that generation, prepared the way for the triumph of the Crescent a little more than a century afterwards.

The Ostrogoths. 8. The more tremendous and equally balanced war with the Ostrogothic kingdom was also a struggle with Arianism. Here the consequences were different, but not less serious, not less affecting the after destinies of the world; for here the Greek and the Latin, while apparently fighting on the same side, were taught to understand their different powers and their different weaknesses, were taught to feel how impossible it was that they should exist together in Italy, unless they were combined by the terror of some third power, or were seeking to destroy each other. Here it was proved how the petty intrigues of a palace might destroy the hard-won fruits of a campaign, and make new conquests, new depopulations, new wastings of the soil inevitable. Here it was proved how those intrigues and the revenge which they provoked might ultimately, through the mercy of God, lead to results the most necessary for the well-being of mankind. How different would have been the condition of the world if the courtiers had not tempted Narses to invite the Longbeards to supply the place of the enfeebled Ostrogoth, if Italy had been entirely given up to the Exarchs and the Popes!

Connection of these victories with the faith of Christians. 9. These *may* be described as victories of the Trinitarian over the Arian faith. The ordinary phrase that they were triumphs of *orthodoxy*, expresses the character of them far more correctly. If we are asked how we distinguish between two modes of speech which are commonly regarded as synonymous, we should answer that to understand the difference between them is the greatest possible help in understanding the age of Justinian. No doubt his name stands with a very doubtful mark upon it among orthodox historians. No one who laboured so hard to acquire the reputation by words and arms, and who was so vehement in his condemnation of others for wanting it, more entirely missed his aim. This is one of the facts in his life on which it is most instructive to dwell. The secret of his failure may perhaps be found in the object of his ambition. The Trinity with him was not a belief, but an opinion. Men were to hold right opinions upon it and upon all other subjects. If they did not, they were to be coerced. But, like everything else in Justinian's mind, this doctrine belonged to the region of decrees. It was true because certain councils, and he the Emperor, who was or ought to be higher than they, had said it was true. Why should men not accept it as much as any edict concerning services or the price of provisions?

10. Herein consists the amazing difference between the struggle for this doctrine as it was maintained in the fourth century by Athanasius, and in the sixth by Justinian. The extracts which we made from the writings of the Bishop of Alexandria showed us what principles affecting the moral being of man he supposed were involved in the theological principle for which he contended; how, in asserting it, he adopted the method which had been a long while familiar to the inhabitants of his city,—which had been marked out by Clemens and unfolded by Origen. The more masculine and practical mind of Athanasius might not be prone to the allegories into which their fancy and their comparative leisure had tempted them; the hard worker might have escaped from some of the idols of the cave to which the student had bowed down. But in all essentials he was, and never shrunk from confessing that he was, their pupil. If what are called the Platonic distinctions were found in them, he inherited them. Had they looked like school refinements, he would have cast them away with scorn: believing the whole world to be interested in them, he clave to them. Arius seemed to him to be confounding the temporal with the eternal —the relations which belong to change, and accident, and circumstance, with those which belong to the divine mind. However he might be charged with indulging in philosophical subtleties, he must maintain that which was needful to vindicate the substance and unity of God,—that which showed how it was possible for the creature to hold converse with the Creator.

Comparison of the fourth century with the sixth.

Platonism of Athanasius.

11. But what was all this to the husband of Theodora? With a feverish, restless intellect; always longing to be busy about invisible as well as visible things,—to be making decrees for

Anti-Platonism of Justinian.

heaven, and earth, and hell,—to be fixing what men should think as well as what they should do, he never seems to have had the belief, scarcely the dream, that anything *is*,—that man can know it, or God can reveal it. Arianism was to him partly the disturbing element in a world which he hoped to bring under the Byzantine rule, partly the disobedience to different maxims which were contained in the *Responsa prudentum*, or in the rescripts of former Emperors, and which might be now embodied in the Digest. Such a man may or may not be a supporter of truths. But Truth is odious to him. He looks upon it as a kind of impossibility. He has a spite against all who have sought after it. If he can detect them in having failed or blundered in the pursuit, his triumph is excessive, his eagerness to pass judgment upon them unbounded, his confidence in his own skill in pointing out the source and necessary consequence of their real or supposed mistakes, imperial. Hence it came to pass that the men in whose school Athanasius had learnt the wisdom which he used against the Arians, were the men on whom Justinian, the overthrower of Arians, invoked such horrible judgments as his generals and armies could not bring upon those whom he thought himself appointed to destroy.

His hatred of all Truth-seekers.

12. There was a characteristic difference, too, in the kind of enemies with whom the poor Alexandrian and the mighty Constantinopolitan waged war. Athanasius defied the living,—the men who had broached the newest and most favourite opinion,—the men who were likely to have the patronage of Eusebius and of Constantine. Justinian, more judicious, sought the champions with whom he fought, in their graves. With passionate piety and heroism, the ruler of the East, the conqueror of the West, poured out his anathemas upon Origen who had aspired to be a martyr in his boyhood, and had lived the life of a martyr to his grey hairs. The man who had done more than all others to promote the study of the divine oracles, the teacher of Pagans, the strengthener of Christians, the converter of nations, of whom his contemporaries could not speak without love, who was most admired by those who were brought nearest the circle of his influence, was pronounced accursed by this profound theologian, for opinions which he supposed he had detected in his writings, of which, whether they were there or not, he certainly understood nothing but the mere outside, and the very worst and most confused of which proved Origen to be a wiser and better man than his persecutor ever showed himself to be in the most creditable acts of his life. The comments of the infidel historian upon Justinian and upon the Bishops of the Fifth Council of Constantinople, who registered his edicts against Origen, Theodore, Theodoret, and Ibas, are instructive

Justinian's war with the dead.

and valuable. "If these men," he says, "were already in the fangs of the dæmon, their torments could be neither aggravated nor assuaged by human industry. If in the company of saints and angels they enjoyed the rewards of piety, they must have smiled at the idle fury of the theological insects who still crawled on the surface of the earth." *We* may venture, perhaps, to ask whether in such company *they* will not rather have wept to think what work these theologians were sent upon the earth to do, and what they were actually doing,—to think, supposing them endued with the gift of foresight, what miseries were preparing for the Church, which was at this moment so inflated with pride and cruelty. *Gibbon, vol. viii. pp. 326, 327.*

13. These observations are a proper and necessary introduction to the subject of Justinian's dealings with the Platonical school. We quoted in the last chapter a memorable passage from Proclus respecting the Platonical Trinity. We purposely abstained from any comments upon it, because it is a subject which should be approached, if it is approached at all, in its relation to the life and history of six centuries, not to the opinions of a particular teacher. We avoided this topic even in our general review of the philosophy, lest our readers should think that it merely formed a section or chapter of that philosophy. It behoves us now to say what we have to say respecting it, premising that it would have been regarded as inseparable by Proclus, by his brethren, and by Plato himself, from that great subject of Unity which "The Parmenides" and "The Republic" bring before us. *The schools of philosophy.*

14. The passage from Proclus can only be looked upon as containing the hint of a principle which presented itself under the most different aspects at different times to him, and to those who were engaged in his class of speculations. His words will teach us that he looked upon a Triad as implied not only in all acts and manifestations of the Divinity, but also in all the deepest thoughts of man and conditions of human life. Faith, Truth, Love, constitute in his judgment a trinity for man. In all the orders of dæmons and heroes such a trinity, or one of which this is the counterpart, is presumed. Proclus takes it for granted always, at times he directly affirms, that if such a triad exists in all the divine manifestations, and in all the subordinate ranks of beings, it must exist in the highest nature itself. Such had been the belief which had been growing deeper and stronger from age to age in the minds of these men; which they thought they could distinctly trace in their original master; and which received abundant confirmation as they became better acquainted with the religions and philosophies of the East, and perceived under what various forms, in countries widely sepa- *The Platonical Triad. Confirmations of their belief.*

146 SCIENCE AND HUMANITY.

rated by space and circumstance, this idea had presented itself; how unconsciously it seemed to have pervaded popular mythologies which were setting it at nought by the multiplicity of their idols; how it had started up again and again in the consciousness of the students who were most embarrassed by it because it looked like a hindrance to their craving for absolute oneness.

How it affected their relations with the Church.

15. Of course in the polemic of the Platonical school with the Christian Church it was a great object to insist upon their possession of this idea. In this case, as in every other, they desired to show that the essential truth was theirs which had been deprived of all its idealism, and adapted to the necessities of the most unspiritual, in the Christian creeds. But however frequently such observations might have been made in the lecture-room, the more intelligent teachers must have been aware that the only hope of victory for them must come from the diligence with which they made it evident that they had hold of a substance and not a shadow. In so far as they devoted themselves steadily to this object,—in so far as they worked with honest scientific diligence to prove that the law which they had recognised was one which governed the facts of the world,

How far a part of Science: how far distinct from it.

and could be discovered in them, they were entitled to the kind of honour which in another region we now render to Davy or to Faraday. But here too they exhibited the uneasy consciousness that human life demands something more than mere laws to regulate it; that faith, truth, and love, if they constitute a trinity, cannot become mere algebraical symbols,—that they imply a believer and an object believed in, a seer and that which is seen, a lover and that which is loved. It was impossible for them to retain a merely scientific position. For what were they to abandon it? The answer has been given already. Their philosophical dignity would have been violated by acknowledging the Christian doctrine. Nay, it ought not to be concealed, there were other hindrances less dishonourable to

The Church becomes anti-scientific as it becomes secular.

them than their pride. As the doctrine of the Church became the established and persecuting one, its most vigorous followers became not only unscientific, but anti-scientific. They were not, like Athanasius, or Basil, or Gregory of Nazianzum, earnest in exhibiting their principle as a foundation for human life. They were merely earnest in asserting it as an accepted dogma. They protested against the Platonists, not because they reduced living truths into abstractions—*that* they were doing themselves; not because legions of intermediate powers were shutting out the Divine Being from His creature—that charge might be proved as clearly against *them;* not because they were a band of exclusive sages hostile to the rights of the people,—they too

THE END. 147

were busy in asserting their own rights, their own notions, their own more paltry and worldly supremacy. The consequence was, that Platonism grew more determined to have a religion of its own, while it grew more incapable of producing or supporting one,—more desirous of asserting its own philosophical idea of a Trinity, while that idea was dwindling into a lifeless notion which had neither outward patronage nor inward force to keep it from sinking into the grave to which all mere notions are destined. [side-note: The idea of the Trinity sustained among the Platonists by superstitions that were adverse to it.]

16. From the other tasks in which we have seen Justinian engaged, we may judge how fitting it was that he should dig the grave for this corpse, and deposit it in its native earth. His business had been with the dead—"man and boy for thirty years"—either to preserve them as mummies in digests, to trample upon them if they had offended him by their speculations, to bury them with all possible indignity if they had no friends to celebrate their obsequies. In the year 529 the edict went forth which drove Diogenes, Hermias, Eulalius, Priscian, Damascius, Isidore, and Simplicius, from Athens into Persia. The reader is probably familiar with the short history of their fortunes, as it is given by Gibbon. As Chosroes was the great antagonist of the Greek empire,—as he represented not only the old Persian empire, but that Persian religion which had been often so closely associated with philosophy, and was always so powerful a rival of Christianity,—these teachers hoped that they should have found a friend, if not a patron,—nay, perhaps that they should discover the Platonopolis which Plotinus had been unable to establish in Campania. But they returned to the Christian world finding it actually less bigoted and less intolerant than that in which they had trusted they should live under the rule of Cyrus or of Zoroaster. Chosroes, however, who, if not the chief of a divine republic, was at least a far better man than the head of the rival empire, stipulated with Justinian that they should live and die in peace. That the history of Greek philosophy may be complete in outward form as well as in spiritual essence, it is made to close, as it was supposed to begin, with a mystical seven. [side-notes: Justinian the grave-digger. The last seven. Gibbon, vol. vii. Their return from Persia.]

17. The historian of the Decline and Fall happily connects the abolition of the consulship with the banishment of the philosophers. An interval of only twelve years passed between the two events, and they are both, though not equally, illustrative of the character of this epoch. The symbols of Roman greatness in government, as of Greek greatness in thought, were to be swept away; the reality of them having long disappeared. But Justinian, as we have partly perceived already, as we shall see more clearly soon, could only sweep away the vestiges of old [side-note: Abolition of the Consulship.]

148   THE LATINS AND GREEKS.

institutions in Rome that he might clear the ground for a more powerful native despotism there; whereas his acts in the Greek world denoted that all its distinctive features were obliterated, —that all its peculiar glory was at an end. Justinian existed, not to destroy, but to declare that the Greek Church and the Greek Empire were withered and ungenerative stocks, from which no more good could be expected for humanity unless some surprising devastation, mocking and subverting all their apparent prosperity, should once more awaken the energy of churchmen and statesmen, and show them that they existed for some other purpose than to debate, to curse, and to lie.

The two acts haye a different signification

18. The famous battles of Belisarius had left Italy feeble and wretched. The Catholic Church, through its heretical champion of Constantinople, had won an apparent triumph in the destruction of an Arian empire which was growing feeble of itself: it sustained a heavy shock by the establishment of a more powerful race of which the king might be an Arian, but of which the subjects were commonly Pagans. If the people of Rome were doubtful whether these barbarians, or the Greek exarchs, were more intolerable, their spiritual rulers at least turned to the monarchs of Constantinople for help and deliverance. But those who had succeeded Justinian were gathering in the harvest of which he had sown the seed. The land which had aspired to conquer the West could scarcely maintain its existence against the Persian. The groans of the Romans, though Popes might utter them, and the Archdeacon Gregory might carry them to Constantinople, were as little heeded there as the groans of the Britons had been, a century before, in the now prostrate capital. They might complain of desertion, but what could their feeble masters do but resign them to struggle as they might with Lombards, with their own oppressive emissaries, with pestilence and famine?

Transition to the Latin world.

Constantinople unable to succour Rome.

19. These well-known facts prepare us for the real separation of the Latin from the Greek world,—for the growth and consolidation of the one under circumstances apparently the most unpropitious, whilst the other was sinking more and more rapidly from prosperity into feebleness and ruin. Gregory stands as the representative of this great crisis in the history of Italy and of Western Europe. From his time the language, however insolent and presumptuous, which identifies the Western world with Christendom, acquires a meaning and a justification: we fall into it unawares, even while we protest against it. We feel that it is the organic part of Christendom: and the consideration of the influences which helped or retarded its organisation; attempts to seize the principle which governed it; hasty generalisations which assume that one part of it explains all the

Gregory the Great.

QUALITIES OF THE LATIN MIND.

rest; and exposures of the fallacy of these generalisations,—may be said almost to constitute modern history. No doubt the annalist is recalled continually to the East; but he is recalled by the report of convulsions which are dismembering it, or that he may observe what wild vigour, what a strong united purpose, is awakened in the nations of the West by the desire to conquer or to restore it. And as it is in the world of action, so, we have hinted already, it is in the world of thought, with which that is in such close contact. The care of documents, the cultivation of a refined antiquarian scholarship, the preservation of the fossil remains of an earlier generation, are duties which the Greek imposed upon himself, which in the main he fulfilled faithfully, and for which we owe him hearty gratitude. The Odyssean gift still remained to him, changed in its objects, but scarcely less strong under the lower empire than in the days of the heroes. He was still, when occasion called for it, the subtlest and craftiest of men. The ambition of governing men, with all the skill in supplanting rivals which accompanies it, may be as much traced among patriarchs as in the clever tyrants in the Ionian colonies. But the energy which grapples with intellectual as with physical difficulties,—the hope which always points to the end of an enterprise, and yet which makes the enterprise delightful for its own sake,—the eagerness to combine and reconcile things which seem most incongruous,—the stubborn toil,—the passion for building, the readiness to begin again when one edifice after another has tumbled for want of a foundation, —the patience which can dig for one through hard rock and amidst frequent inundations; these are qualities for which we look in vain to the successors of Solon and Thales, and which we find, with all their accompanying extravagances, follies, tyrannies, rebellions, in the world which rose out of the ruins of the empire of Augustus.

How the Western world comes to be regarded as Christendom.

20. The accomplished historian of the Middle Ages, in his work on the Literature of Europe, speaks of Gregory I. and Nicholas V. as aptly represented by the Night and Morning of the great Artist. Such a comparison comes naturally and gracefully from a refined scholar, who not only sees in the banishment of Greek literature from the Western nations an unspeakable loss, but connects with it the formation of a barbarous Latin tongue, and an incapacity to appreciate those who had spoken it in its purity. Still more naturally does it belong to a defender of moral and intellectual freedom, who has good reason to think that it was crushed under a system of government and dogmas which Gregory inaugurated, and that the surest pledge of its recovery was the revival of that classical tone of feeling which Nicholas patronised and helped to diffuse.

Night and morning.

See Hallam, History of Literature, vol. i.

But as annalists of philosophical inquiries, we must demur to the sentence which to a judge who contemplates the subject from Mr. Hallam's point of view appears so reasonable. It is not our present business to canvass the merits of Pope Nicholas. We hope we shall never be found disputing the necessity or the ultimate blessing of the social change which he and the Pontiffs who succeeded him deemed it judicious to encourage. But it is important that we should state our reasons for *not* believing that Pope Gregory was an instrument in shutting out daylight from Europe, and plunging it in darkness.

Probability that Gregory disliked letters;

21. We should wish our readers to understand that they are not bound to agree with Mr. Hallam on this point because they may entirely agree with him in his opinion that Gregory was an enemy to classical literature in general, and to Greek literature in particular. Controversies on this subject have been raised by learned countrymen of Gregory, jealous both for his reputation and for the cause of letters. But without considering the special pleas which they may urge on his behalf, we may admit that those who, with Mr. Hallam, reject them as unsatisfactory, have the strongest *primâ facie* evidence on their side. It is in keeping with all we know of the character of Gregory that he should be jealous of Pagan teaching, willing to substitute the legends of saints not only for the most living fictions, but for the best histories which they had bequeathed. As a man of business, occupied in raising his city and country out of physical and moral degradation, he could have had little leisure for any studies but those which directly belonged to him as a priest, or a priest-legislator. His unfriendly relations both with Greek emperors and Greek patriarchs were certain to confirm his Latin prejudices. As a converter of Pagans he would be anxious that the lore which they received should be that which was contained in the Scriptures, or had originated in the Church. As the organiser of forms of worship which were to bind the different parts of Christendom together, he would wish that they should have as little as possible to remind them of other kinds of worship which civilised nations had adopted, and which had given a colour to their thoughts and writings. It must require some very decisive documents indeed, to show that a man with all this internal bias, and all this power of outward circumstances driving him in one direction, did in fact take the opposite one; that in spite of himself and of his age he encouraged studies which he had every motive to discountenance.

and yet was a great instrument of promoting education.

22. Still his intelligent apologists must have felt that they had some reason for their opinion. They must have thought that Gregory did in some remarkable way contribute to the

intellectual education of Europe, that they should be guilty of ingratitude for all their own advantages if they denied it, that they were bound even to strain facts that they might establish it. Without any straining of facts, we think their position, when so stated, is capable of the most satisfactory defence. Was it not necessary for the education of the West, that it should be left to work out a course of thought for itself? Could the classical writers have been worth anything to it at this time? Was the enthusiasm with which they were welcomed in the fourteenth and fifteenth centuries merely the rapture at the discovery of a lost treasure? Was it not the consequence of a discipline and preparation which enabled them to perceive a living sense in that which was actually dead to the Greeks, who could construe, admire, and criticise? What that discipline was, we hope we may be able to point out hereafter. We have hinted already, that a portion of it was such as amply to revenge any injury that was put upon the old Greek masters, seeing that it was under one of them, even in the most imperfect and distorted medium, that the Western scholar imbibed the knowledge which he thought most precious. But our present business is to show how Gregory led the way to those philosophical pursuits which he would himself perhaps have regarded with more jealousy than even elegant literature. What homage the Middle Ages paid to Greece.

23. The first feeling when one contemplates a man who, becoming Pope at the moment when Rome had reached its lowest point of depression, succeeded by his gracious and unselfish government in leading the people to hail him as their deliverer, and the best of all civil rulers,—who, finding so large a portion of Europe Arian, brought it into a united fellowship, —who began to draw into that same circle so much of what had been previously heathen,—who, without the command of any of the swords which Justinian wielded, won triumphs for the Church far more extensive as well as far more durable than his, —is certainly one of wonder, if not of gratitude. But this feeling is quenched in the minds of a number of Protestants by the conviction that Gregory was establishing a uniformity of opinion, of government, of language, in countries which could only expand while they realised their distinctness; that the opinions were such as concerned the deepest mysteries, and therefore, whether true or not, could have no practical hold on the people of the countries in which they were established, and could contribute nothing to their moral development; that the government, nominally paternal, was of that worst kind which rests neither upon the worth of the man nor upon the dignity of the family, but only upon sacerdotal assumption and the ignorance which upholds it; that the language was one which Apparent greatness of Gregory.

Why Protestants dispute it.

had not the least pretension to be universal, which was hard and ungenial, adapted to laws and forms, unfitted for the seeker of truth, prized only because it excluded that one which was richer and freer, because it would submit to all barbarous innovations from the theologians who wielded it, or from the native dialects which it held down.

These are heavy suspicions; some of which at least we must have a strong disposition to entertain; each of which requires to be seriously considered before we can know whether Gregory was a benefactor or a curse to mankind, and before we can advance many steps in the philosophy of the Middle Ages.

Gregory's orthodoxy not the same in kind with Justinian's.

24. When it is said that Gregory sought to establish a uniformity of opinion in Western Europe, and that to a great extent he succeeded, the words should be carefully weighed, or they will lead to serious confusion. He was not occupied about opinions, as Justinian was. He did not habitually look upon Truth as the sum of his tenets or holdings. He might very often, indeed, act and speak as if he did. But those experiments which he made to produce a common worship in Europe, expressed his true mind much more than any dogmas which he uttered. He desired that the Name into which Christians were baptised should be the object of their common adoration. To unite them in *this*, not in certain intellectual conclusions and definitions, was assuredly his main object. He sent his

His leading idea.

missionaries to tell pagans that an invisible mysterious Being was calling them from their different idols to serve Him. He bade the Arians acknowledge that there was an Eternal Son, one with Him, in whom they might approach Him. He declared that the whole family was united by one Spirit. Whatever theories he might add to these proclamations, here was the root and substance of them. Whatever superstitious importance he might attach to the forms in which he enjoined that the worship should be celebrated—however much he might sometimes overlook the diversities of character in his old or new disciples,—this was certainly the idea to which everything else in his mind was subordinate.

The objection that his faith was mysterious.

25. Hence we think it is obvious why the faith which Gregory proclaimed was necessarily in mysteries. It was not that his own mind had any natural affinity for the mysterious. It was hard and practical. Whenever he invented or decreed, he showed how much he clung to the visible, how ready he was to indulge the pagan propensity for it, how much he was disposed to reduce the Eternal and Infinite under the conditions of Space and Time. But by making the worship of the Divine Trinity the foundation of the Christian society which he was doing so much to build up, he was counteracting this tendency of his own

character, he was making the difference between the old Heathenism and the Gospel which he diffused, to consist in this mainly, that Pagans were scaling Heaven by different earthly ladders, making heroic men the grounds of their conception of the divine; that he was putting forth the divine Name revealed in Christ as the mysterious foundation of a Catholic society. The question whether in doing *this* he was checking human thought and inquiry, or whether the hindrances which he and his successors certainly threw in their way, did not arise from their doing something different from this—the direct opposite of this—from their canonising the old Heathen methods, reversing the one which they confessed to be the Christian one— must be determined by the facts of the history. Some negative help has been afforded us already for the formation of a judgment on this point. Without resting overmuch weight on the fact that the most enlightened and tolerant of Arian monarchs was the persecutor of the mild philosopher Boëthius, we have sufficient evidence that the Gothic and Vandalic monarchs, though often far more generous and truthful than their orthodox opponents—though supplying an element in European society which it could ill have dispensed with,—were not favourable to intellectual cultivation. Deriving from the teachings of the excellent Ulphilas, whose simple mind had been formed under the influences of the age of Valens, an impression that Christ was a higher Odin, an illustrious demigod, they probably accepted as much of the Christian faith as they were able to bear, and in the way that was most suitable to their previous discipline. The effects were genuine. The best side of the old character, the love of truth and plain dealing, was brought out. If the new faith did not displace the sottish habits of the old savage, if sometimes it threw a darker glare over his crimes, at least it made him feel the majesty of law, confess the might of weakness; at least it enabled him to quicken the corpse of Roman civilisation. But the belief in heroes, even in a transcendant hero, if it gives energy to action, does not lead to meditation. The visible world fills the Goths with a wild wonder, and they long to conquer it. The battle brings forth a number of thoughts greater than they can master, respecting an invisible world which is about them, and one to come which must be the counterpart of this; the confusion may be expressed in legends and poems, in which the critics of after days try in vain to separate the Pagan from the Christian elements. But the hope of any clear light upon the mysteries of our own life and being, the desire to explore them and arrange them, has been the result in Western Europe of another faith than the Walhalla faith, or than any modification of it.

His inclination anti-mysterious.

Mystery his safety; love of the visible his danger.

The Arians unfavourable to philosophy.

Their merits

The Christianity of the Gothic and Vandalic tribes.

Hero-worship unfavourable to thought and reflection.

THE IMPULSE TO PHILOSOPHY.

Schools in England the result of Augustin's mission.

26. To show that Gregory, with all his own alleged indifference to letters, was a greater instrument in promoting education, in the strictest sense of the word, than all his contemporaries or predecessors, we need only examine the condition of England in the century after it had been brought under the influence of his missionaries. Schools seem to rise as by enchantment; all classes, down to the poorest, (Bede himself is the obvious example,) are admitted to them; the studies beginning from theology, embrace logic, rhetoric, music, astronomy. But these facts, though decisive as to the awakening influence of that faith which it is sometimes assumed must have put the world to sleep, concern us less than the directly philosophical impulse, which we must trace, if we follow plain evidence, to the acknowledgment in Western Europe of the mystery that had formed the subject of conflict for six centuries in the East.

Philosophy occupied with the Trinity, though not as in the Platonical age.

The questions to which it had given birth during that strife would naturally take another form; there were no longer Neo-Platonists to speak of a Trinity as ideally true, implied in the existence of man and of the universe, while they disputed the actual revelation of a Trinity; no longer eminent Christian teachers to vindicate the doctrine, both as law and fact, from the impugners of it among themselves and in the outlying world. It had taken its ground among recognised principles embodied in common acts in which king and peasant had an equal interest, asserted by edicts though not deriving its authority from them. But because it had this position it awakened questionings just as the sight of an actual firmament, and the presence of an actual sun, lead to astronomical inquiries which

Awakens inquiry not less because it is accepted as true.

would scarcely be pursued if men had only the dream of a possible firmament or a possible sun. Whatever we may suppose *à priori* might or must have been the case, our *à posteriori* experience enables us to affirm that the Trinity did become the starting-point for all the metaphysical and all the moral philosophy of modern Europe. What different forms these inquiries took; what fears they excited; what efforts were made at different times to suppress them; why these efforts necessarily failed, we shall have to explain hereafter. What we say here

The philosophical impulse could not be checked.

is, that no uniformity which Gregory was the instrument of producing, or which he wished to produce, in the least availed to hinder all possible ethical controversies and all metaphysical controversies from arising in the most or in the least reverent minds; in those who were most disposed to acquiesce in the decrees of Popes, or in those who were most fretted by them. What we say further is, that the mystery which lay beneath his desire for uniformity, because he believed it the basis of unity among men, acted as a counterbalancing power to the Latin

THE PAPAL GOVERNMENT. 155

love of rules, forms, dogmas, and compelled him to ask with as much ardour as the Greek had ever done, what constitutes right, order, obligation among men; under what eternal laws they live, think, speak, act; how they are connected with the physical world; in what respect they differ from all the other portions of it. Ethics and Metaphysics connected with Theology.

27. We may be suspected of greater reluctance to deal with the second subject to which we referred, that of the government which Gregory was the instrument of binding on the neck of the Western nations. We do not for a moment dispute that he, more than any other man, consolidated the Papal power, and defined the limits within which it could be exercised. We are willing enough to use the favourite *argumentum ad hominem* of Protestants, that he denounced the title of Universal Bishop as profane, but we cannot forget the occasion of that denunciation; that he quarrelled with the assumption when it was put forth on behalf of the Patriarchs by John the Faster; and that therefore his very protest was a link in the chain which was to hold the Latin nations together, and to fasten them to the chair of the successor of St. Peter. That protest; the separation from Constantinople, of which it is one among many indications; Gregory's earnest faith; his deliverance of Rome; his missionary zeal; his freedom from the ambition and secularity, to a considerable extent from the arrogance, of earlier and later Pontiffs; tended, beyond all doubt, to make the assumptions which they might only have been able to express through bulls and anathemas, veritable facts in European history which cannot be gainsayed, whatever may be our judgment about them. That judgment, we believe, will be distinct and satisfactory only if we are willing to acknowledge the experiment to establish a fatherly or patriarchal government over the nations as the most important and interesting of which there is any record,—an experiment which could but involve the deepest truth and the direst contradiction if there is such a fatherly government already existing, and if there is a struggle in man not to acknowledge it. The records of the way in which that truth and that contradiction gradually made themselves manifest through the struggles of the ecclesiastical power with the civil, of the catholic body with the particular nations, belong to general history. But the schools, as always, in their own way represented the world. The subtlest metaphysical questions respecting the individual were involved with questions concerning the social and political, condition of mankind, which after-ages would have to unravel. The limits of Obedience and Freedom, of the Universal and the National, of that which is and that which is enacted, of Faith and Reason, were forced upon In what sense Gregory established the Popedom on a new basis.

The Papal experiment.

Its place in history.

156   THE LEARNED LANGUAGE.

Its effects on philosophy, metaphysics, ethics, and politics. the minds of men by that mighty effort to create a sacerdotal tyranny, which Papists and Protestants seem agreed to confess was almost entirely successful; while the documents to which both appeal prove that no spiritual or secular terrors and punishments could in the least quell the opposition which it excited, and that it took its shapes of good or evil from those who apparently submitted to it.

The one language. 28. Finally, when we speak of the one language which Gregory, by the forms of devotion which he sanctioned, and by the general character of his missions, did so much to establish as the organ of spiritual communication in the world over which he reigned, we must crave liberty to notice one or two points which Protestant polemics and classical scholars are disposed to forget, but which for our purpose (and, we think, for theirs also) require to be seriously considered.

Uses of a sacred language. 29. It was the existence of a language which did not belong to the market, which represented higher thoughts and feelings than those with which men were commonly occupied, that made the tribes of modern Europe conscious of their spiritual necessities, and of the powers which there were in their own native tongues to express them. The idea of a school,—of instruction and education at all in the higher sense,—was inseparable from the existence of such a medium. Moreover, the Latin operated continually as the third power which mediated between two contending tribe languages, and ultimately enabled to mingle in some higher. The law courts and the palace did not succeed in making the French of the Normans or the French of the Planta-

The Latin cultivates and preserves the native languages. genets triumphant over the Saxon of our people. The ecclesiastical Latin was a common object of reverence and fear to both. Ultimately it helped to bring the strong elements which suited the immature life of our forefathers, into an organic English. Its despotism, then, however severe, however mischievously protracted, was not really injurious to any people who had native strength to encounter it; their old language received its impression, and grew to be a living one, adapted for the highest moral and intellectual purposes, by means of it. But what chiefly concerns us is this: It was the prevalence of this school language, though uncouth, distasteful to the modern man of refinement, hard to manage even by those who wielded it as their ordinary instrument,—nay, by reason of these very qualities,— which determined the peculiar direction of the philosophy of the

Character of Middle Age philosophy determined by the use of the Latin tongue. Middle Ages. The familiarity with which we speak our own dialect makes us forget to ask ourselves about its words,—to inquire how far they are distinct from the visible things or the invisible realities which we connect with them. They become dangerously identified with that which they express at one time, dangerously separated from it at any other. But we do not question them to know how they are related, or how they are separated; we can scarcely put them at a sufficient distance from us ever fairly to present the puzzle to ourselves. The schoolmen of the Middle Ages had these questions thrust upon them: they could not evade them. After ages might laugh at their folly for raising such doubts. But they did not raise them. There they were, demanding resolution. To pass them by would have been ignominious cowardice: they could have no satisfaction on other points till these were settled. And they had this compensation for the sneers of their descendants: they were contributing in innumerable ways to clear difficulties out of our way; to make it unnecessary that we should often travel the ground which they explored; to point out the track when circumstances call upon us to revisit it; to make it possible that we should enter upon inquiries of which they knew nothing, and yet which they fancied they could settle by their methods. We apprehend that our obligations to them for the clearness and precision which they have been the instruments of giving to discourse; for the hints which they have supplied us respecting the laws of thought; for showing what they could and what they could not do,—would be as cheerfully and cordially recognised by our learned and honoured countryman, Mr. Mill, as by the most fanatical reviver of mediæval notions and practices.

The realist and nominalist discussions of the Middle Ages.

Why necessary.

www.ingramcontent.com/pod-product-compliance
Lightning Source LLC
Chambersburg PA
CBHW051106160426
43193CB00010B/1333